Accosting the Butterflies

Selected Persian and English Poetry

REZA BARAHENI

Translated By: Aleca Baraheni

BUTTERFLY ART HOUSE LLC

DEDICATION

I dedicate this book
To my wife, Sanaz
  And my children:
    My daughter Aleca
      My sons Oktay Mohammad, Arsalan, and Esfandiar
        My brother Rassoul, my sister Ashraf
and in memory of my oldest brother Dr. Mohammad Naghi Baraheni, Professor
of Psychology who established Educational Psychology in Iran
and in memory of Zahra Soltan and Mohammad Taghi, my parents who taught
me the discipline of hard work in the service of humanity.

Reza Baraheni

TABLE OF CONTENTS

AUTHOR PREFACE

Selected English Poems

AUTHOR PREFACE

Accosting the Butterflies is a translation of a collection of poetry published in Iran in 1994 by the same title, 'Khatab be Parvaneh ha'. The book was a revolution in contemporary Persian poetry as I introduced Postmodern Persian poetry. Poetry should use language itself to speak to our thoughts and desires by being multilingual, polyphonic, and deconstruct language to use a multiplicity of fragmented forms, sounds and descriptions, free of any constraints of form, rhythm, and narration. Influenced by Persian and world poets, my poetry reflects on repression, the longing for a homeland, love, loss and the yearning for freedom. In addition to poems from the original book, Accosting the Butterflies, includes translations of some of my later poems and some of my English poetry.

In the 1970s, I accepted an invitation by the University of Iowa Writers' Workshop to teach in the United States. While teaching and lecturing, I met and immediately became good friends with Allen Ginsberg. We were both very interested in human rights and social justice. We had a few poetry readings together. In those years, my books, *God's Shadow: Prison Poems (Indiana University Press, Bloomington - 1976)* and *Crowned Cannibals: Writings on Repression in Iran (Random House, Vintage, New York - 1977, Introduction by E. L. Doctorow)* were published about my prison experience under the Shah of Iran. Years later, when Allen passed away in 1997, I was deeply saddened by his loss. My English poem Requiem for Allen Ginsberg and the article I published in the Toronto Star in 1997, *Remembering Allen Ginsberg*, are both included here in this collection as I recall the occasion when Allen introduced me to Jorge Luis Borges.

One of the great elements in the writing of Persian poetry, at least in my process of writing, is that you never say no to a poem, because it appears in its own angelic guise of dictatorship. You cannot help but embrace it, and it engulfs you in a dream. You are, I tell you, doomed to write the poem and even rewrite it many times, until you either give up or the poem gives in. Whenever I opened the Bible, the Quran, Rumi's and Rilke's sonnets and the poetry of Hafez, I found that all great poets of the world are primitive, classic. When I opened my mail and read the poems of my former students who attended the writing workshop I ran from the basement of my home in Tehran after the current government banned me from teaching at Tehran University, I recognized that poetry has no gender. It receives all and is the trickiest espionage of the universe into the emotional lives and dreams of all creatures. It has its own gender and genesis, and it is the greatest espionage into the affairs of the romantic, modern, surrealist, realist; Homer, Dante, Shakespeare, Nietzsche, Ezra Pound. How can one differentiate one poet from another, and of course, I mean one real poet from another real poet? There is no other definition for the poet: The poet is a poet is a poet; insane and sane at the same time; Moslem, Christian, believer or atheist, all at the same time.

The poem that suddenly invades the mind, interrupting almost everything in a blind search for itself, hardly knows where it is going. It actually appears to lead the poet, rather than the poet dictating it to the typewriter or the paper. In its early stages of composition, whether it takes the form of a short piece or a longer one, a poem becomes independent of the world and even of its author. It becomes so independent of its primary authorship that it chooses its own author, as if the poet who is actually writing the poem, has been hired for the mission of delivering only the poem at hand, absolutely different from any other prior piece of poetry written by one's self or anyone else. Singularity and difference are concerns that determine whether the poem is going to be different from any other poem, regardless of any barriers, social or ideological.

Translator's Note:
In translating poetry from one language to another, every effort must be made to preserve the linguistic characteristics of the original version and the intent of the poet. In the effort to render a poem from the original version into the target language, the poem appears to go through a tormented test of survival in the destination version. Since the poet is my late father and my most precious mentor, I had the good fortune of having his input at my side, every step of the way for this collaborative effort. For this, I am most grateful. This collection of poetry includes translations of some of his most famous poems, known for their experiment in language and lyricism such as 'Did Not Come', 'I am Addressing You Beautiful Lady Iraneh', 'Losing Consc…', and 'The Whirling Gaze'.

باغ و دریا

روی برگِ تو درختی: باغ!
روی یک قطره باران: درخت
من نوشتم: دریا دریا!
و در آن لحظه زنی
چشمهایش را
به کلمه‌ها بخشید.

رضا براهنی

به رسم یادگار نظر شود برای سعادت، الهه و یحیی مازندرانی، نوه‌ها
از اولین مصرع از رضا براهنی

The Garden and the Sea
You wrote on a leaf: Garden!
I wrote on a large raindrop: Rain! Rain!
And in that moment a woman
Bestowed her eyes
On the doves

One of my first poems handwritten in Persian on the left as a memento during a visit with my daughter.

Internal
A steel star has sat me beside the moon
And no hand can pass through this architecture

April 26, 1990

Mouth
A strange thing remains awestricken by the mirror
The shape of a mouth screaming
To retell an ancient and tumultuous dream
But the disabled tongue
Has blocked the scream

When will the day come for us to hear the scream?
Hear it all?

October 29, 1990

Woman-Shaman
Riding the bird   and
Descending from the star   and
Penetrating the tree
Reaching the bottom   to
The bottom
To the bottom of the sun   and
Returning   to
The back of the bird   and   the Woman-Shaman!!

October 29, 1990

The Temptation of Questioning
For Maftoon Amini, the poet of the heart's wisdom

A horse stands by the window behind the colorful leaves
Its taut back   arched   under   the spell of the height of beauty: You
From the sun-speckled autumn sky   dream and desire   pour together
Is it a memory?   Is it the memory of love?   What is it?
My voice returns from the corridor of leaves and the tunnel of the
                                                        season's tempest

Wait a minute
I don't have a handkerchief
After I wipe away the torrent of tears with the back of my hand and
                                                        sleeve
And hide my bloodshot eyes in the pockets of my wet eyelids
And after I swallow the dry wooden gulp in my throat blocking my
                                                        breath, I will depart

Later   When I lie asleep under the weight of a white stone
I will come back to you like the spirit of obsession in a breeze
I will remain there by the window
With all the passion and excitement of watching
And this question:
And now   In that small lonely room that hides the moon in its four
    walls, [like a woman hiding her past beauty], what are you doing at
                                                        nights?

I am quite sure I will receive my answer
Because posthumous questions   are never left unanswered

December 7, 1990

Fountain

The fountain was about to flow up high into the endless white
Suddenly the doorbell rang   You said: "Oh, my mother!"
I said, "What happened? Where is she? What did you say?"
                        "He slowly passed by the steps again!"
"Oh, my mother!"
And the doorbell rang again
I saw that Shahriar[1], passed through the network of associations
I saw:
On a circular flag, a woman   on a circular iron, a woman   on a
                                        circular glass, a woman
On a circular kiss, a woman   on a circular breast, a woman
                        on a circular essence, a woman
On a circular knee, a woman
In a world of insane concentration of unity and multiplicity dancing,
                        happy, whirling
And then a tree fell from the sky of kisses   in the bedroom of bodies
                                thrashing about
The fountain erupted into the endless white

Now   the fountain sleeps on the bosom of the sea
And Shahriar the fish
In the network of associations

December 8, 1990

---

[1] Shahriar – Seyyed Mohammad Hossein Behjat Tabrizi, pen name, Shahriar, was a notable Iranian Azerbaijani poet who wrote both in Azerbaijani and Persian. His most important work, Heydar Baba Salam is considered to be the pinnacle in Azerbaijani literature which gained great popularity in the Turkic world and was translated into more than 30 languages.

The Moon
For Mohammad Nouri[2] and His Great Voice

That felicitous insanity that was robbed of me
— Using the tactics of the trickster dawn that was fickle —
I turned into a prophet   rejected by his god
His prophetic tongue blocked
I am that hell whose pains   you repeat in your dreams
The sun is a round firewood within me
A constant burning   always with me
And my eyes are the ashes from the depths of which
            The phoenixes of the world's pain are born
I am alone
Ever since   that felicitous insanity of mine was robbed of me

Now it is I
The man who got lost in the world's deserts
The man estranged to the ports of trust and reconciliation
Drowned in the waters of a thousand distant gulfs
A prophet who knows no sleep

Ever since her happy tall shoulders   closed   closed   the world's
                                                           beauty
That heated cooing on lovers' balconies
The spring of whispering that slowly crept   in the dawn
                              of my mind's ears   closed
The soft loving touch of the pick on the beautiful tar[3]
                              in the evening   closed
The world's darkness is what I deserve   what I deserve is the world's
                                                        darkness

Carrying the mourning flag
A strange moon passes above the night
How can one's spirit stand
the tragic memory of destruction!

Look!
This is forever!
This watching of corpses!
This parade of unwashed corpses   under the moonlight

---

[2] Mohammad Nouri – One of the foremost folk and pop singers in Iran.
[3] Tar – Long-necked, waisted string instrument, shared by many cultures and countries
including Iran, Azerbaijan, Armenia, Georgia, and others near the Caucasus region.

under the mourning banner!
The horse neighing in my dreams   is a horse without a rider
A horse mourning in deep sleep   Under the moonlight

I had a pact   with the bright Milky Way of the future
                                on the expanse of solar cities
Now look at me!
I have turned into an ancient city
A corpse under the heat of the desert sun
This sub-structure of jaws and teeth
After all, how will the world rebuild me?
This is eternal
This image of the corpse   This old city   unwashed

Carrying the mourning flag
A strange moon passes above the night
I recognize it
It is my moon
A moon carrying the wound of an infected catastrophe
                                across its chest
A hungry wolf has grown wings and is flying after the
                                moon in the sky
This is not a dream
I've seen more ominous nightmares
I've seen it during the day, while awake
The starving wolf ever devours   ever devours

A flood
          Slapping, roars on and comes
                    across from you
This flood will take the entire sub-structure of the jaws
                    and teeth of the city, this ancient city
And dumps it into the mouth of this shark of an ocean
Beneath the water   the shark swallows   time
And gives birth to the timeless, colorless seeds in the water
                                in the coral archipelago

With the colorful eyes of a parrot   whose colors
                                she poured onto her tongue
And imitated love   I am in love   from the true dawn of
                                lovers
By the tactics of the trickster dawn that was fake
My felicitous beloved was robbed of me

A strange moon passes above the night
Carrying a mourning flag
Look and see!

November 12, 1990

Accident

Out of the spring of dove and leopard   Out of the abrupt feeling of
            objects and the sky   the sun's cradle emerges
Time: three hours before the rise of the face   or five centuries away
                                                from the sea
On the white deck of the ship   under Solomon's sails   hundreds of
                                                corpses oscillate
The length of vision, internal   a few millennia
The Kheder of sails upright   tender sailors   underneath the seas of
                                                death
Women of laughter in the blossoming map of dreams hanging from
                                          astronomical months
Then the angel of death screams, "Charge! Hell is our target!"
We charge forward
Tales and myths pour from our shoulders on earth   from the
                                          rooftops of oblivion
We scream in a forest of branches turned into piles of ash
We forget the gods
Phosphorous, star, monarchy, tyranny   all or none
These are accidental
If I had seen your eyes at the moment I had set my eyes
                              on another woman
I don't know what I would have done   Maybe
I would have slept in another galaxy at the age of emotions and kisses

The angel of death screams, "Hell is our target! Hell is our target!"
I am sleeping under the water with your dream inside the shell,
                                    inside the shell

December 12, 1990

Breeze and Ash
For Poet Javad Mojabi

The ashes lying on my chest from you   are hot   still
Through the alleys, barefoot men carry the corpse of a deer upon their
                                        shoulders   as they pray
And school kids only slightly taller than dusty stray cats   remain
                                                awestruck
The walnut eyed passersby   are hollow   a slight pressure of
                        fingers   will break them
Then   the blind impasse   will swallow   the sunlight of the world

There is blood running down the green alleys of my autumn
                        the wine in the cup is foaming poison
Polluted from the root, yes   polluting the earth was at its root
The goodwill smile of the cupbearer   will finally deceive me
This is clear   one day I will bottoms-up the wine

Yes, it passed quickly   that millennial day of wonder   upon which we
                ascended to the Heavens from the cross
–Paws blooming like a red rose   a sky filled with singing stars in
            our throats   heads surrounded by an illuminated halo
                                                thirsty–
How poor the present age is!
Our corpses are rotting like crumpled newspapers in the remote alleys of
                                                the world
One day I will bottoms-up this cup   I will bottoms-up
The cupbearer's goodwill smile   will finally deceive me

Oh breeze, oh, you don't know   there was a day when the tempest
                        trembled   fearing my eyes
Now, like the last autumn leaf   I have a fever   I tremble in your cold
                                hands   It's not fair!
If you want to take something   take away the ashes upon my chest
But you had better know that you will turn the horizons into a bloody
                                                spectacle
When you pass through the gardens of swallows
And the green leaves of the world   you will make them tremble

It is hot   still hot   your ashes   upon my chest

December 24, 1990

Speech
I always scream with my mouth shut
But you always   hear my screams   with open ears
My screams stay between my mouth and ears

January 3, 1991

Even If The Voice is The Last Voice of The World

I cannot sleep
The curtain is drawn aside and I cannot sleep
I have fifty-five holes instead of a throat   fifty-five throats—
          fountains of blood   every throat – a whirlwind of light
Fifty-five windows   fifty-five lovers
I sing this love   with all of my throats
I have fifty-five women   standing by windows
I have fifty-five sacred names   that I repeat nightly
Fifty-five secrets in bloom   call fifty-five women to fifty-five windows
The curtain is drawn aside and I cannot sleep

The women are asleep by the window   and the sun   has just risen
The dew evaporates from green sprawled pastures,
          awaiting the footsteps of fifty-five fifty-five–year-old children
Fifty-five clocks on the wall are ticking and the dots of whispers connect
                    with the waves of rumors hanging upon shoulders
The fifty-five-year-old heads and manes and tails of horses appear before
                    me through the windows of fifty-five stables
When the silver beards of fifty-five-year-old men   occupy fifty-five
                                                  mirrors,
Fifty-five red female drums   beat down hey haay   hey haay
Then the whistles of water fairies   the collective dreams of
                                        suns call out
Fifty-five ships come near riding the breasts of fifty-five waves
It's the eyes of revelation in the ports   that recline before the sun
Because
In the shallow bed of that gulf   there is a burning eye wide open
                              under the water   weeping gold
Fifty-five abundant soapy tresses of women   under warm showers
The slippery soap slips away   from the hands and flanks
Then the musty scent   the scent of fifty-five moons and deer navels
                    evaporate from the crevices of fifty-five doors
A melted eye is open: trickster painters wash women with
                                        the colors of the sun
Fifty-five pairs of eyes of illumination   swallow   their bodies

I drew this strange circular continent   with my long binoculars
     from the ship of my early morning sleep   I drew closer and saw,
                                        bewildered

Now   sleep has escaped me   in the spring of a fifty-five-year-old lover
A fifty-five-year-old rainbow   is growing from the world's breakfast tray
The clouds of morning birds   are always presented to us

in fifty-five-year-old mornings, beheaded and bloody
Beheaded men who call-out when they come to welcome me
Now: fifty-five suns of no good mornings   fifty-five fallen moons
    fifty-five years of goodbyes   fifty-five-year shadows that are
                                                    being filled
Fifty-five scattered autumns   fragmented autumn of days gone to the
        wind   under the saddles of fifty-five women on horseback

I cannot sleep
I saw your eyes for a moment   I cannot sleep

Once a star that swiftly passed through the night called out to me:
"Fall in love! If you hear my voice again you should know that
                this is the voice of the end of the world!"

I cannot sleep   I cannot sleep   I cannot sleep
Until that star calls me again   even if that voice might be the last
                                    voice of the world

The dove by the window   the fence by the empty bench
                and dream, the dream of the legendary parrot
The face, a dowry of brazier fire
And the kiss, kisses from your eyelids, and the needles of stars,
    that passed quickly through the night and called out to me:
                                    "Fall in love!"

I cannot sleep
Now   Sleep has escaped me   in the spring of a fifty-five-
                                year-old lover
I saw your eyes once   the veil was removed   I saw you
                                for fifty-five years
I cannot sleep   until that star calls me back again   even if
                    the voice, is the last voice of the world

March 10, 1991

What I have Written
For Aleca
"And the other dedication is for that angel, upon whom no demon has any influence."

From Shams-Tabrizi

The names of all the birds in my dreams   I have written for you here
The names of all the ones that I have loved
The names of all the good poems I have read
And the hands that I have shaken
The names of all the flowers   in a blue flowerpot   I have written for you
here
When you pass through here   take a moment to look under your feet
I have written the names of your feet as well
And your arms when they become bridges to love and butterflies, and
      embrace the doves and pigeons   I have written for you here
I have planted a circle in the garden, that the sun lights up in the night,
and the moon in the day
And a falling star traveling through the universe   has grown from it
I have written its name here for you as well
Forgive me   I have been away from you for many years
But always, whatever I have seen, day and night, anywhere
And whomever I have kissed   I have written for you right here
only for you
Far away, but in total attachment;
A large bird, in its nest, I am resting from fatigue;
The spirit of all worry, eyes awaiting you, focused;
The mysteries of all the wandering tribes, I have written for you here
Sadly, the youth who climbed the dirt roads with me are gone now
I know each and every one of their names
And I burn from remorse   when I read each name
They were all the children of our hopes and dreams
My interpretations of their dreams are repeated everywhere
I have written the interpretations for you here as well
In the gardens   some of the middle-aged trees have been
weeping for years
Because the wind has swept away the nests of their swallows
I have told people to light young candles around the trees
The names of the middle-aged trees   the names of all the swallows
I have written for you here

And the dead were of two kinds
I have lifted the curtain from   the dead
Look closely now

One group never seemed to die
As if their phosphor bodies were returning from the cemeteries
And lit the cities
They were the light of the future;
And the other group   was innocent
As if they had never been born   as if they had died from the start
A large underground broom was sweeping their dust,
Pouring their remains in an endless pit
This sweeping back and forth was the essence of nature
I have written the names of both groups of the dead for you here

I would have loved to have laid a beautiful face   on my chest
                                                  and died

But this did not happen   and will not happen
Existence is stingier than this
Look at the life and death of Hafez
The way Hafez lived was a relative affair
We never understand how Hafez died
As if he had carried away the closed fist of his death
                              like a hidden tradition
Now, as you pass through the ways of the world
Look into those deep pits I was forced to crawl through
These pits have circular openings
If you look down from the sky, the opening of each pit resembles
    an old daf [4] with holes driven into it by the daf-player's fingers
But   behind the walls of these pits   a daf is being played also
Kurdish dafs
This is how I have travelled from the earth to the sky to visit the sun
–inside an ancient daf   when the daf was being played all around me–
The world is meaningless for me
I would have loved to have laid a beautiful face on my chest   and died
But this did not happen
Existence is stingier than this
The pain a sensitive person feels is immeasurable
I have also written for you here a summary of the beginning and
                                                  the end

Although my soul is ravaged

---

[4] Daf – The musical instrument is one of the oldest large frame drums played in Iran
and neighboring countries. The Persian and Kurdish dafs are used both in spiritual
rituals and entertainment gatherings.

But, my mind is the strangest thing
Saying these things has become more difficult with each passing day
I am not the Hafez of all time
But even if I die   I will never forget anything
A lifetime has passed never to return   everyone's life, not mine alone
I have planted the memories of the world and humans   in the circle
                                                 in the garden
The circle   in the garden   was the product of the essence of my life
Each fruit falling from a branch of a tree, falls into that circle
Is repeated in the circle
Repetition and interval, repetition and circle, the repetition of circles
between intervals
Were the fruit of the essence of my life
That circular outlook too I have written for you here
Now   come closer and take the key to the garden from me
The address of that garden   on this key   I have written for you here
I have been away from you for years
And I am going to sleep
I have drawn the curtain aside
Now you can roam the garden peacefully   like a butterfly
                                     with absolute ease
I have also written for you here   the wings of the butterflies
                                     with fresh colors

October 30, 1992

Departure and Return

She came to me   with her black and white herd of rabbits
She came to me   with a young dove's cooing in the
                                    soft morning throat
She came to me with her body thrust as an unsheathed sword
She came to me   she was sleepy   she was awake   wherever
                                        she was on earth
It was the tomorrow of the next hour
The yesterdays of the day of resurrection
She came to me   hundreds of thousands of light years from
                                        the future
She came to me   the reflection of universal femininity
                        in the moonlight of the East or West
Like cities of memories   such as Khiva, Balkh, Samarkand
                Ray, Shush, Parsa, Bokhara   she came to me
She slid down my cheeks   like my tears
She slept on my chest   when she woke up and went out the door
                        she came to me the following night
She came to me   with the warm scent of her flanks   with her
    crescent heels   with the scales of her full moon shoulders
                        strong and tall burning of her throat
In the privacy of four insane lips   she lived with me
            with her eyes   she died with me   but, she still
                                    came to me

Her fingers   being my pens
When she came to me   she put her smooth tall fingers in my
                                    feverish hands
She would say write!   write and write again!   of my wood,
                    or my flame, or my ashes   write!
Then she would leave   wandering in the misty space of day
                    and night spreading her beauty
And she astonished the eyes of the world   with the candelabra
                    of her elbows, her wrists, her ears
With her mouth   she bestowed the world   like a kiss to
                                        the poor
She went around wandered and again   she came to me
And a hundred thousand magnetic clocks   she went around
            beating, and gave me tidings of her knees, of her ways

When
She came to me

January 6, 1991

See
A tall poison the height of a cypress tree gracefully entered
$$\text{the port's gate}$$
A tent of blood the size of sails erected itself
My ship seemed to be in love with the whirlpool
It moved and hid in the disarray of the waters and the wind
They saved me from the waters on the other side of the world
Drunk and upside-down   mute, deaf, and blind
I stomped my foot on the ground asking where is my port,
$$\text{my tall poison?}$$
My fever is making me pass through the pit of the sun's oven
See my ashes!   Come   See my ashes!

January 29, 1991

Spring

Spring has come, I am sensitive
I am a running tempest of coughs and sneezes among the daffodils
I am sensitive
I have shaved my beard
My mustache is the color of ancient mountains
And my lungs' tears stream from my eyes
I have kept only a vague trace of the wintry snow on the crown
                                                    of my head
And my back throbs in pain and the fingers of my right hand
                                        holding a pen, tremble
It is not old age my dear! Not seeing you has made me so sensitive
And from the other room   a voice says in his sleep, "Dad! Dad!"
I am sensitive
A storm of sneezes and coughs among the daffodils

March 30, 1991

Did Not Come

I hurried   so that the sun would come
                 It did not
I ran after someone insane who had poured her oak tresses on
         the warm magic marble of her buttocks
                          so that the sun would come
                 It did not
I wrote on paper, wall, stone and soil for people to read
                          so that the sun would come
                 It did not
I howled like a wolf   I ran pushing my muzzle into the belly of time
         I tore into it   I tore into it night and day
                          so that the sun would come
                 It did not
What a strange evil pact!   The age owning the dog, I, its dog
When I was driven out of the house   I leaped into the house from the
                   roof of devotion   so that the sun would come
                 It did not
I slapped my face several times in the seclusion of my home
When I walked into the street
I held my cheeks   like two burning steels before the people
                          so that the sun would come
                 It did not
Although my sobbing at night from bitter dreams, awakened
             the children of the world from their tired sweet sleep,
But, I could not cry
Not amongst friends   not in the presence of strangers   nor alone
            I could not cry   so that the sun would come
                 It did not

April 29, 1991

Broken

Decayed   Decayed   The evil autumn of such beauty
It poured on our world   a thousand and one
                 a thousand and one nights of disgrace

A woman crumpled   the four corners of the world
               opened the window   and tossed it away
Although   the sun of her eyes wove a thousand carpets of
              golden threads in a stranger's garden
But how she left the medallion of our hearts half-finished under
           creation's feet   how she left it half-finished!
How soon we fell from the grace of the world!

What a sad refraction   your clear tears from behind the
                    dusty windows
This very ill-omened break of light   continues in the other
                     phenomena
The mulberry tree   that very galactic and secure umbrella of
                squares broken
Wine does not shine out of the prison of its carafe
And the tearful voice of Delkash the singer   reaches the ear
           in fragments from the old record of youth
And a broken sitar   is sitting   by the trashcan

Decayed   decayed   the evil autumn of such beauty
It poured on our world   a thousand and one   a thousand and one
                   nights of disgrace

June 7, 1991

Accosting the Butterflies

My days and nights passed through the green corridors of your cypresses,
             devoted butterflies of past and future
The bastards who were pillaging my moons from the skies, seasons and
           lovers' verandas   are surrendering now
Behold now! I am rolling alongside an army of young whales
The light of the scales of ocean fish   opens up the landscape
In the musical plain of thousands of singing sharks   I bring the world's
            crimson whirlpools to dance
And the trout staircase of my eyes   always brings the beautiful passengers
          to the galaxy of my new explorations
The universe's bats   whirl under the eternal light
But I have created a new sky   with the love of young suns
I will not conceal from the sky   the fact that my eyes have seen everything
A split moon passes by the clouds   a double-edged sword without a
                 handle
My eyes have seen everything, yes, everything
The bastards who were pillaging my moons from the skies, the seasons
         and lovers' verandas   are surrendering now

My days and nights were passing through the green corridors of your
      cypresses   devoted butterflies of past and future

I will hide from human eyes, one day   or like that Roman God
Or like my fellow countryman Shams   I will die in a suspicious,
          symbolic, and bold tumult
All of you, stand there with open eyes among the spectators, I am lunging
         forward alongside a pod of young whales
My eyes have seen everything, yes, everything

May 29-31, 1991

It Seems As If The Dream Is Not The Same Dream
When I leaped from under sun into the shade, I saw that
                        the shadow was not mine

Returning
I saw that the sun was not the same sun
On the border of the sun and shade
I saw that a pair of five-hundred and fifty-year-old sycamore trees of
Anis-Al-Dawla[5] were turning a woman around at the speed of a whirlpool
And the woman screams behind the leaves, and no one is there to drive
 away the ghosts of Saghaffi[6]'s house from behind the paintings of the
                        master painter, Mozayyan[7]
From underneath the hundred-year-old tiles, the termites have slid out
And they are climbing up the books of dreams, spirits, and fantasies
And no one knows where the birds are
And the woman screams from behind the leaves
I saw that the Shah, standing outside Saheb Gharaniyeh
Palace of Niavaran has put his hand in the hands of a trembling hag
The pair of five-hundred and fifty-year-old Sycamore trees are watching
                        Saghaffi bewildered
The hour is all the hours the hour is all the hours the hour is all the hours:
The old and dead men of a few millennia ago hands across their chests,
                distressed and helpless are standing in line
On the edge of a five-hundred and fifty-year-old carpet
And this silk square   blows up all its colors toward the circular air
                an all-seeing atmosphere rains upon the colors

When I tell them about my dream   I see   it seems that the dream
                                is not the same dream
When I leaped from under sun into the shade, I saw that the shadow
                                was not mine

Returning
I saw that the sun was not the same sun
The viewer is gone   the hour is all the hours   only the atmosphere of
                                vision remains.

June 24, 1991

---

[5] Anis-Al-Dawla – (1842-1897) The title meaning 'Companion of the Sovereign' was given
to Fāṭema-Solṭān, the most important wife of Nāṣer-al-Dīn Shah Qājār of Iran. She was
the only wife who spoke her mind openly and criticized the ruler publicly. She
accompanied Nāṣer-al-Dīn regularly on his travels.
[6] Saghaffi – Surname
[7] Mozayyan – (1846-1932) Aliakbar Mozayyan-o-Dolleh was an Iranian artist who was
born in 1846.

Open the Window!
How did these eyes of mine benefit from yours after all?
The sound of crying came from dead gardens
And then it subsided   I felt cold
When I shut the window, I turned around;
But the flicking of a distressed finger on the window pane
                              made me turn around
I looked out the window
Two men made faces and gestures, saying, open the window!
When I opened it I saw that they had left a heavy-set corpse at
                              the entrance,
And they departed   I shut the window
Now   I have a good time with this corpse
The sound of crying no longer comes from the gardens
After all, the corpse is my own

June 29, 1991

Kindness

One by one, I counted the violets of the plush green and respectable
Mr. Life
Only a few violets are left for me to count at the end of the garden
I know that I detest the parrots whose ghah ghahs and kagh kaghs come
                    from the corridors of the fancy, noisy parties
I hid like the hoopoes in the jungle surrounding Bizhan, Mansoor, Akbar*,
                    and their wives and children in Astara
No one will be able to distinguish me from the clouds, the sky, and the
            shadow of terrifying trees that sleep in the swamp at night
I used to think that one day the future will lift me on its shoulders with its
                                capable hands
But what a terrible mistake I made   There was not going to be a future
Now, I am only thinking of Bizhan, Mansoor, and Akbar whom even if they
                    open their doors and windows
Even if the entire sea passes through their homes
To drive away my voice from the homes of kindness and attachment,
                    I will still find my voice reflected there
I will return there again
And kiss the apples of the kind eyes of Bizhan, Mansoor, and Akbar
Only a few violets are left for me to count at the end of the garden
                            and then I will leave
No one will be able to tell me apart from the clouds, the sky
    and the shades of terrifying trees that sleep in the swamp at night

July 2, 1991

The names mentioned in the poem above belong to three fellow poet friends of mine living in the city of Rasht, Iran with whom my family and I stayed and had a wonderful time. Their names are, Bizhan Kelki, Mansoor Bani-Majidi, and Akbar Exeer.

Presence

All the things I have known and hold dear should remain a memory for
                                            another time
Two windows   two verandas
The bridge drawn into the eyes of the night by the wings of thousands of
                                            ducks
Stars appear in our eyes through the flapping of those wings
And the wind, that strange wind from which the sun flows towards my
                                            chest
The fence of a garden in spring from which flowers pass hurriedly on the
                backs of moths through the delicate wings of bees
And things resembling these   and like women who lead us to the roads
                                            of ecstasy

The truth of the matter is this:
That my legacy from my time is nothing more than the black nature of this
                                very word, "Mordeh Reeg."*
Be bolder than I
Distribute the stars of the world among women
That in my time, women   did not even get a simple light of a distant star
Deliver the key of Elias's existence to the hands of the world's children
Because you witnessed the pleasant scent of the doves
Don't build cages
So that lovebirds and canaries can fly to your windowsill on their own
When the world turned into a flower
Transformation took over   and you grew wings overnight
Remember me
I who was always in love with the ascensions of the ancient East
Remember me   when young newlywed brides are giving birth to their
                                            children
I will be present   by their beds   and at the birth of a wave of a
                                            satisfied smile
And in all the kisses   my lips will be present
Time passes so quickly   my death is a millennium old
All the bridges I destroyed and passed, you build, destroy, and move on
And be kind to the woman who killed me
That this beautiful crime, was always welcome

Even if a hundred thousand years pass   ask for me again
Ask for me from the depths of darkness
I will be present at your table
In the form of a window, a curtain, or the smile of a cloud

don't be afraid
When my throat explodes
Because I will remember the history of the universe   and the history of
time
You ask for the first narrative   or the last   or any narrative
Don't be afraid   Because my wings are made of the same material
as your dreams
Don't build cages to keep me your captive
The cage is the sign of fearing the violation of flight
Sit me by the window
Ask me: of what was and what will be
I will read to you in the form of what has been read

I will read in the name of the throats of your loves
Don't be afraid   Ask

July 29, 1991

*Mordeh Reeg —
Mordeh — Dead
Reeg — Sand
The combination means legacy

Admiration
Your clap awakens universal doves in me, an earthly being
How can I clap when I have no hands?
But blossomed be my lips that kiss at night the half-moon profile of
your face
Take my eyes away for having dreamt of yours!
Let me see you, where are you, your face a garden blowing from
a thousand windows of light in the morning?
And your shoulders there what white clouds on the height
of which the crown of a face, a sun!
How can I clap when I have no hands?
How can I clap when I have no hands?
Tell me where you go when dreams go on vacation and we turn
to crying and crying turns to us, where?

And what is that shadow behind you on the night that my poetry is
following your steps
What hands you have   resembling kisses!
And when the earth is brimming with you, look what a plain there is
when it is being combed by kisses and the breeze
Which hand has sharpened you into a reed with such perfect curves
Like a kiss you have such green fingers!
Don't leave
Tell me where you go when dreams go on vacation and we turn
to crying and crying turns to us, where?

Stay!
How can I clap when I have no hands?

October 24, 1991

Oh, Those Few Seconds, Buster Keaton!

Fifty-five years ago when I put on the shoes of the world
The world started to turn like   a movie reel   in a vague and dusty
                                            atmosphere
I ran like the actors of silent movies before I was born
Proud   and at incredible speed
Fifty-five years ago

But you, love! You seem to hurry away to the other world
                      fifty-five years and a few seconds ago
Like a mother dying a few seconds before the birth of her only child
And the child is healthy, but, what kind of healthy!
Without a mother to have set him upon her lap   and kissed his cheeks
                                  and licked his hands
And later, everyone points out: "Your mother looked exactly like you!
                                an apple split in two!
And they showed me the album of the lovers
Like the pictures of a dead mother shown to you after a
                thousand months when you are breathing your last—
Like the drafts of love   without there being any signs of the love itself

Oh, those few seconds, Buster Keaton!

October 29, 1991

Elegy

That the moon looks at the moon
                    Why?
Never looks at me
                    Why?

That upon the neck held high   the head of the beheaded sun
                    Watches the world so well
                    Why?
She never looks at me
                    Ah
                    Why?

That she has scattered the galaxies   from the tops of her flanks
                    Towards everyone and no one
                    Why?
She never looks at me
                    Ah
                    Why?

That in the silence of her lips rest all the mysteries of the earth
                    Why?
She never looks at me
                    Ah
                    Why?

And water passes before the mirror again
                    Ah
                    Why?
That tip of a dagger of deep fear is held to my chest
                    How sharply this sorrow tears me apart
                    Why?

That the moon looks at the moon
                    Why?
Never looks at me

                         Why?
She never looks at me
                         Ah
                         Why?

And water passes before the mirror again,
                         Ah
                         Why?

November 4, 1991

Fall in Teheran
It began   at first   a strange whisper   in the wind and among
                    apparently young green leaves
Then sick sneezes arrived   from happy street children
                    who lay in bed a few days later
Describing the looks of people of this kind   alone
                    only fits minds in love with music
When the wind blew, it stirred up deep tears in the weak eyes of
                    retired old men in the parks
As if an eternal tragedy had rained upon their cheeks
The women hurried   the people in line grew restless   shivering
In the wind   the apparently young and green leaves were watching
                    them   wet and eyeless
And they consoled them in bits and pieces in their deficient faulty
                    language
In deserted streets   young lovers   placed their shoulders upon
                    the hollow of their lovers' chests
– It suddenly got cold!   I am cold!   Aren't you cold?   I'm cold
                    are you cold?
– No!   I'm still hot!   Hot!   From kisses, hot with your kisses
                    still   still...–
Then an unruly crow appeared in the horizon   it pulled a knife
                    toward the sparrows
With the curved hammer of its beak   it pounded the ways of
                    the air
It cawed: the season of burning space is arriving   I am your
                    king!*

The pillage of the branches started at night
As if there was no end
They fell in the luster of the rain and wind   under the street light
Hundreds of thousands of colorful, small, wet scales dropped
                    from the sky onto the earth
Bare-headed men with no umbrellas walked with newspapers
                    shielding their heads
Night drove the water down the drains   from the bright North
                    towards the world's South
And the next morning   the alleys of the world were full
And the fresh scent of the season's opium rose   from the leaf
                    piles
A strange siesta stole the world away
In the boring hour   the arrow of the haggard Fall man
                    penetrated the stream of death

And the next day in Darakeh[8]
When a young woman   showed me the sun that had just shone
        upon the festival of the death of color   I was weeping

I was not accustomed to seeing so much death in the world
The sun came from every angle and direction
And threw a huge ship of leaves   from the boulders of Alborz
        Mountain, as if pouring them   into the waters of my eyes
The sea of my eyes   wept blood   from the colors of the leaves
Oh season, season of insanity deep in a dream! Oh sleep, sleep,
                        the sleep of insanity in the season of water!
Oh yellow leaves   pouring upon my shoulders   when I no
                                longer exist!
I wept
—Without being able to make sense of so much destruction of
                                swollen dimensions—
My loving peacocks   beheaded   floated away in the waves
                                of water
And a wayward parrot from a hidden sky   imitated the sun
I wept
—Without being able to make any sense of this all

Who is this who is coming from the sidelines   alone   burning
                                lost?
The woman of this shaman? The poet's mistress?
No! No!
Put on the clothes of the death of love   on the body of the
                                young leaf!
Bury it!
Have the corpse's ashes thrown into the wind and water!
I was not accustomed to seeing so much death in the world
Without being able to make any sense of this all

December 2, 1991

*I am your king – Referring to a line from the Persian poet, Mehdi Akhavan
Sales in his poem, "The King of Seasons, Fall"

---

[8] Darakeh – A neighborhood located in the northern provincial capital of Tehran, Iran.

34

Shorra
I was so in love yesterday
The child of your happy eyes
When you stood up straight   screaming non-stop
I love I love I love
Then sat down saying nothing
Only from the happy corners of your almond gaze   the sun glowed
A pair of fleshy eyes below your shoulders   naked   watching me
And they closed my eyes
So that my ecstasy would carry me to the arms of your streets
The scent of acacia the touch of brush   in the depths of
                                maddening waters
And
To be pulled up like waves on a moonlit night
And the return, and the fishlike spine
And the salty perfume of being sheered away from you when a heated
        confusion flared up between my knees and my heart
A horse like green coming from a star descending to that hall
                            of silence
And I, calling out god, god, so that the world would not end
And the spinning of time and earth would continue forever
Like this you, being crystallized in that other
I was so in love yesterday
More than always and today
A man like the alphabet of mystery with buckets of water, taking
        ablution during the day before the people in the square
And people rush from all the streets
To make that huge parrot chest of his rise in the mirror
Shorra sharayah shara shahoorra! Shorra sharayah shara shahoorra!
Yesterday I was so
Much more in love than…
Just like you who in that very…
Shorra—

January 21, 1992

I wrote this poem when I was a Visiting Professor at Oxford University.
The title of the poem is only a sound. It has no meaning. The lines at the end
of the poem are also sounds. They have no meaning.

Passing By Again

An angel is passing through my street again
In the old crimson cup, a human mirror seems to pass   again
From the white chirping of the throat the soft fingers of Chopin
                              pass the piano keys   again
Tears that sprinkled on the face
Sobs that explode now
The magic of the color of oak   on top of the cypress tree
And fingers of persimmons   and human and mirror pass   again

January 27, 1992

Image Summer

On the screen of a swamp on fire
A veil of jasper mosquitoes change direction
A bit farther   a garden of tulip bubbles exploding mortar-like under
                                                    the Western sun
On top of the heated fingers of sycamore trees   the thimble
              over-brimming   with the colors of parrots, mynas,
                                                    and the sky
The crystallization of the sieve of needles in the eyes of swallows
This: sky;

But the earth was another story
Under thousand-year-old mulberry trees
The scent of fresh tea from the tea gardens   brought the scent of
                                        temptation and perfume
We exchanged kisses – like happy children exchanging mulberries with
                                                    butterflies
Fingers sweet
Lovers' whispers – wealth blown in out of thin air – ears filled with
                                        dizzying markets
Unlike others, we were setting our imagination in the cells of
                                        memories:
Swords' play of your ancient tresses on my chest
My side torn-up by your lips
When your fingernail slid down my shoulders
It seemed that   Michelangelo was drawing David's image on
                                        my face
The dimensions of geometry all became distorted
The geography of a smile over-brimmed from your eyes
The power of your youth felicitated my eyes
And bursting into laughter   blew in the light   like a winding
                                        highway

An angelic thief stole the virginity of the world
And an angel was pressing her lips into a juicy pear

This was your face sleeping on my chest   or the moon –
                            gardens bursting with fruit

Lighthouses had come together in the tumultuous festival of
                                        seaports
I was with you like a barrel in a garden   assaulted by violent hail
from every direction   secretly engulfed in pleasure

This first and last word, given more thoughtfully:
I never found a whisper   benefitting the people of the world
                                        except that of lovers

The world is hanging us from itself like a caged poetess hanging
                            from the heights of a galaxy:
Like the brilliant lowering of a huge chandelier in a great party of
        rowdy children, without inflicting even the tiniest scratch
                                        on anyone,
After the fall   only   one sentence runs through everyone's lips:
                                        this, is a miracle!

Yes   we have fear and pleasure together
And no one can separate us

September 21, 1992

In this Strange Beautiful Land
Today, I was reminded of your kisses
In this strange beautiful land
And your short crescent hair   Short or long? Or parted in the middle?
                                        I don't remember!
And your hands
And your shoulders
And that luminous oblique of your eyes
Something between black, hazel, and date
With no gender?   Maybe all   I don't remember!
These are not all of my memories
They are only reminders of the distance
The collection of distances are my memories of you
                    or yours?   I don't remember!
Are you one person?   Or a collection of people?
Or a combination of absolutely accidental references to all the
          dear faces I have known?   I don't remember!
Are you my childhood?   Or my old age?   If I were a woman
                              would I be you?
All of these thoughts combined randomly in my mind in search
    of the geography of you alone or the geography of all of you
But it seemed that I was not lacking anything   I was overflowing
And I was taking you from where you were sleeping beside me
                carrying you to the old horizons of my memory
Even now, they are not my entire memory
As if I were a landscape, watched by the people from a distance
Around me   a veranda of people's eyes
As if I were a road through which my people pass day and night
For me, people, mean those I have known
I was a native jungle where my people slept at nights
And greeted each other during the day
I had nothing to do with all the people of the world
For me, people, means those I have known
For me, people mean you, the jungle of yous
In this strange beautiful land!   What am I doing here?
Today, I was reminded of your kisses
Your part in the middle?   I don't remember

You were sleeping here beside me
But I was seeing you in the old territory of my memory

Today
A hand slowly opened the hidden window of my chest
They awakened you inside me

(I wish they would always awaken you inside me!)
Suddenly, from behind the caged bars of your dreams
        I was calling out the world's jungle like a huge bird
And I was getting wet with the rain of your soft hair on
                                    my shoulders
I had no umbrella to hide me from the pouring of your dreams
They were pouring on me
(You've seen how we sometimes want to hide in the smallest
                                corner in the world
Like a dove hidden between the fingers of a magician while
                    its heart is beating non-stop,
Then at its most vulnerable moment, from the open fist,
                            it takes flight)
I wanted to hide   in your birth place
That small hidden birth place   that creates a dove out of thin air

It was pouring on me
You were asleep   here next to me
I was taking you somewhere else you were sleeping there by my side
Are you one person?   Or a collection of people?   I don't remember!
What are you made of?   How were you made?
        Are you silken or made from somewhere beyond the clouds?

It was pouring on me

Flying saucers
Have flown from you towards me   From the past to the present
Do they arrive today? Or when?   Tell me!
I am thirsty
When will your jug in space turn green?
When will you set the table for a hungry one like me?

Here, the women are all whirling   on the satellite or anything else,
                                they're all whirling
But I want the moon, the moon, the moon!
Like the warm greeting of your face   the forest of your hair
                            from the depth of darkness

I miss you   Even if you are sleeping here beside me

In this strange beautiful land
Without you
My soul
Like the tomb of the unknown soldier, was empty   empty and

ceremonious
Who cares for the respect of total strangers?
Suppose they sacrifice their God before my feet!
So what!
I was dying
I wanted you to see what I was doing
As if a hidden loudspeaker   kept whispering your name
                                        inside my soul
I wanted my soul to come down from these trains, airplanes
                                        and ships

And sit on my shoulder
Hide me in your birthplace
Without you I saw everyone   but no one saw me
I was alone in all the stations of the world
In the winds, all the books of the world kept opening and
                closing   someone was reading them
I was not reading anything   and no one was reading me
On the subway, everyone was reading, going, coming, and reading
I was left alone among them
And the loudspeaker kept repeating your name in my soul
And nothing in the world was mine
What's the use of respect from strangers?
Suppose they sacrifice their god before my feet
What good does it do?
When you are asleep and the other yous are asleep!

Everything has its own rule
Except love
And it seems that love has no rules

You were standing on the other side of the rails
With eyes on the other side of the galaxy
With your hands across your chest
And your purse and suitcase on the bench
The entire world passed between us
Like a neat and organized jungle
I wanted the world to fall apart
I wanted to leap down from the world's skyscraper
And the loudspeaker kept calling your name

And the rails and wheels of the trains and airplanes kept whistling
And the crumpled bodies sitting in the cabins　　seemed to have
　　　　　　come from other planets　　they were strangers
I wanted to say that if this is the world　　it had better disappear
　　　　so that you and that jungle of yous only remain for me
And the loudspeaker kept repeating your name or your names

And then　　in the final assessment
A hand slowly closed that small hidden entry
And the loudspeaker turned off
I
Jumped down from your sky
Or your sky jumped down and I remained up there　　alone

In this strange beautiful land

I had carried you so far back into the past that it seemed as
　　　　　　　　　　　though I no longer knew you

Everything has its own rule
Except love
And it seems that love has no rules

February 9-11, 1992
Oxford, England

Haah

We are always building new cemeteries   but
Look at my heart that belongs to those ancient cemeteries whose
                              graves are being sieved into the earth
Time has put the world into a sack
And suddenly someone arrives   from another millennium
And places a stone, a cover, and an identity on the grave
And standing before it   arms crossed   stares at the stone
                                        weeps   like myself
The daf of my heart will rise to dance from those cemeteries
Halam halam hala lam lam halay halhala halhal
And he cries in my native tongue and eyes
Because weeping is original   to this language   to these two eyes
Halam halam hala lam lam halaay halhala halhal
And passed the night, passed, who was it? Was it the nightingale?
Or a flower? A flower? Halay halhala, a flower, a flower
Take my arm, my flower, if you are drunk!
Halam halam hala lam lam, take my hand, if!
And then someone suddenly comes along   like myself
A daf-player, a singer, in the gardens, at the foot of the mountain,
At the foot of the mountain, finding your picture, secretly
                              embracing it hard, saying,
"My language! My language, my poor wasted language!
How my beautiful mother tongue, how it burned inside me, absolutely
                    turned into ashes   like myself   myself!"
Time has put the world into a sack!
Time has put the world into a sack!
Hold my arm, my flower, if you are drunk!
I hugged her: "How beautiful you are!" She said, "Don't say that,
                    swear on my life, that you won't say that again!"
"You will never die, never, and I will never part with you, never!"
                                                    I said

And she wept
Wept blood
"Your eyes are sieves, my flower, gold is being sieved out of your eyes
With those tears of yours, I feel soaked in blood!"
She said, "Swear on my life, that you won't say that again!"
She said, "Swear on my life, that you won't say that again!"
"Hold my arm," I said,
"Hold my arm, my flower, if you are drunk!   Like myself!"
Halam halam hala lam lam halay halhala halhal
Halam
Hala
Haah

Let Rudaki[9] play the harp!
Let the son of the Balouch come and play the delicate lute!
Let Shahryar pick up his tar and sit by my side
And may Haj-Sadegh sit across from me with his daf
And let Paveh go to Zabol, and Balkh come to Tabriz
And let the music of all instruments start, continue and remain,
And then I will say, "Haah!   hala   halam halam hala halhal
And now it happened as I had said
It happened as I had said
The players look at me
When I am at the end of the garden, I secretly press that
                                                    picture against my heart
And now it happened as I had said
We wept blood all of us
We all wept blood
The daf of my heart will rise to dance from those cemeteries
The daf of my heart from that grave
And you listen to this land!   A thousand years!
You hear the sound of music from this wasteland!
                                                    A thousand years!

Someone pressed an old picture of yours at the end of the
                    garden and wept   haayhaay   like myself!
A thousand years
Halam
Hala
Haah

Dadamdadamdadamdadaghoorghod   we said we said
                                                    all of us
And hand into hand hand hand hand into hand we gave
And we shut down all the roads   for a thousand years
All of us   wept blood   all of us   for a thousand years
Halam
Hala
Haah
Haman

December 31, 1992

---

[9] Rudaki – Rūdakī, byname of Abū ʿAbdollāh Jaʿfar ibn Moḥammad, (born c. 859, died 940/941), the first poet of note to compose poems in "New Persian," written in Arabic alphabet, and widely regarded as the father of Persian poetry. One hundred thousand couplets are attributed to Rūdakī, but of that fewer than a thousand survive.

This poem was written in Turkish, my mother tongue. To get a feel for the
sound and rhythm of the poem, here are parts of the poem in Turkish:

va oonda man diyaram: Hah! Hala halamhalahalhal
va indi man diyan oldi. Chalanlarim manah bakhsin
baagin dibinde o aksi basanda bagrima gizlin
va indi man diyan oldi
va indi man diyan oldi
chalanlarim mana bakhsin
bagin dibinde o aksi basanda bagrima gizlin
va indi man diyan oldi
gan agladoukh hamimiz
gan agladoukh hamimiz

The Seventh

Today is the seventh day of the absence of love
I have spent   the night by the window with meaningless fears
Cats were on guard   under trees filled with fearing swallows
What was happening to you down there, underneath the young soil,
                                        the perfumed soil?
Cedar tresses were tattooing my body all over
Was I dead, polluting water, light and air?   Or you,
Who had bestowed the fragrance of your body to the earth?

Last night: a night like a hundred-layered double-chins with
                    hundreds of bloody stars hammered in

The nightmare descends
We pour rose petals on your tomb   we shed tears
A beheaded peacock hangs from the eyes of the crowd
What is happening under there with your cheeks? what?

A perfume that stupefies
A perfume that wiggles in our dreams, in our horrifying nightmares
Bestows your fragrance onto the world's spirit

The marble that had the perfume of tuberoses and the tresses
                    of the moon melting into termites

We pour the flower blossoms on your grave   we cry
                                        we return
We return alone and empty-handed

October 22, 1992

After the Visit

At night   we ate   the snow   with the leaves   with the sun
                                                              together

Do you remember?

We went   on horseback to the fields of dreams
Do you remember?

I said: Do you have any hands?

—I don't remember

I said: Spring has ten graceful fingers
From her melancholy-hued eyes   stories ooze
Those eyes: the space-of my-chest-saw-Buddha
Do you remember?

—No! I don't remember

And then
Upon an ancient kilim, I slept like a God

February 21, 1993

We Are Burning
"The eternal return of the same" Nietzsche

Under the protection of whose wings are we flying today?
Who do we see on top of the waterfall?
Who is it that is waving at us   from the bridge?
Whose rainbow is it that bends from the friction of the waterfall with
                                    the sun and our wounds?
From whose precipice has the fawn fallen off?
And those really good and red apples have fallen off the branches!
                                    Why?
What are these worms doing to the flowerbeds?
Whose day is it today?
Under the protection of whose wings are we flying today?

These paths, these paths,
Whose paths are these stretched before us so perfectly, whose are they?
                                    Tell me!
Whose paths are we taking?

Yes   sometimes   we feel we have arrived
But when the sweat of hot paths have cooled
Far away   subjectively   they seem to be changing the stage for the
                                    invisible spectators to watch
We realize that we may have come too fast
As if we have passed the location where our arrival was to be
                                    announced
Yes, we always got off past our stop
–Beyond the summits and the heart of the precipice,
Beyond the flower beyond the woman beyond the perfume of a
                    woman's hair   beyond that young person–
How did we pass through the summits the summits the summits?
It seemed that they were ringing the bells when the caravans pass
                    through only after their fall
And they were turning the stage for the invisible spectators to watch

–Very well   now   what must be done?–
When we insist, they say, "Very well, don't say,"
Go back   to the beginning of the crossings
And
Start from that cross-section where a hundred thousand drunken
                                    rails pass through!
Perhaps this time, will be your last–
But how?   We passed through the summits!   And you had

                                        Sounded the bell!–
–No!   Return!   Perhaps you will reach the destination without
                                                    knowing!–
We say: We won't say, "Very Well" because the stage has been
                                                    mixed up
But tell us   who is ruling today? Whose summit are we on today?
            and from the safety of whose wings are we jumping?

Oh summit!   We see you in our dreams   Do you also
                                    see us and our dreams?

Before the discovery of notes, we were playing songs
                            and the guests were clapping jubilantly
Before the arrival of notes   we were being applauded
                                before the arrival of the first note
And we were running   before the arrival of the first notes
                                                    for the feet
The secret of our failure is in our strategy
They said: –People drink water instead of pure alcohol and they
                                                    get drunk

But you?   what's this got to do with you?–
Nothing   very well then   we're just talking–
They said –Don't say "very well"–
We won't say   We run like mad everywhere   and don't know
                                    the meaning of fatigue

Oh summit!   We see you in our dreams   Do you also
                                    see us or our dreams?

And the scent of female hair is destroyed
The fawn falls off the cliff
How have the suns blinded your eyes   oh fawn?
And the galaxy of your view is empty   oh fawn!

And then we thought the end of our running must be the
                                    beginning of our flight
When we wanted to get up from the ground
We noticed that we had been running in our place

We said: –Very well   running in place is something to do

They said: –Quiet!   we said: –We didn't say anything to you!
They said: –Strange thoughts passing through your mind, such as
                              – "very well" we didn't say–
They said: –Quiet!
Then we saw that we were dancing a strange dance
In the same way that before learning the notes we were
                              playing songs on the instruments
And the quests were clapping and dancing
We were dancing on the hot sands   we danced before jumping
Like trained and engaged horses   we danced   and the guests
                              laughed

And blood penetrated the hot sands
Our heads capless   all our pants loose   skirt in hand
                              the weight of duty on our backs
And the sun reflected the desert pans from its depths
We were dancing on the desert pans
We were screaming that we had better and better deeds ahead
We haven't had the time to converse with the gardens, the flowers,
      the rivers and the sea   we haven't had the time to
                              speculate on life, the moon, and time
The rebirth of the sea of world memories   is a waste of your time
They said: `your words don't make sense! do you understand our
                              language?–
We repeated our words
We were both misunderstanding each other
We said: – we are having a conversation–
They said: –ants have or used to have conversations with each
                              other too
We said: –Pardon us but these words of yours are comprehensible
They said: –These words of yours   even their being comprehensible
                              is incomprehensible–
We said: –Very well   we will not say anything –
They said: –This too is totally incomprehensible
                              don't say "very well" either–

These desert pans these desert pans this dance

Until the wind blew, the sky roared: –Where is the end?–
And then a tall wing came   we hung on to the wing   and rose
We never asked: Under the protection of whose wings
                              are we flying this time
We took off
And a world of mixed lines beneath our feet was screaming and
                              being destroyed behind us

At the speed the world was going, it seemed that it was going to
                                   to be gone forever
When we thought again that we had arrived once more, we noticed
        that we had gone beyond the location where our arrival
                                   was to be announced
At the heights above the waterfall   a white hand was still waving
And they were ringing the bell
The bridge was closed and the hand was waving   and they were
                                   ringing the bell
The fawn was bouncing off the cliff into the valley   and they were
                                   ringing the bell
A rainbow was sprawling behind us   and they were ringing the bell
We placed our scorched feet on the burning sands
We said: –Say no more   we will say ourselves that we will never say
                                   "very well"
And we return   to the beginning of the cross section of beginnings
So that once more we can set-off from that cross section where
                      hundreds of thousands of circles fade into
                                   one another
Now   we drink water instead of pure alcohol and get drunk too
What are these worms doing to the flowerbeds?
These desert pans these desert pans this dance

We apologize but this point must be made:
One day before sunset they threw a beautiful woman from the sky
She seemed to have been asleep at the beginning of her fall
                                   from the summit
We saw that   she woke up in the middle of earth and sky   and
                                   she tried to sleep again
But the awakening from the fall did not give her a chance
She fell on the roof of a dove's castle
Hundreds of birds set her on their wings and took off
And the scent of the hair of a woman was blowing in the wind
                      at the cliff with the wing
Then a young boy emerged from under the rocks
Ageless, pure, beautiful   face glowing   black eyes
When he saw us, he said, "what are you doing here?
We said: –Our ritual of dancing on the desert pans has ended
We are just burning now
He came, stood and watched us
We said: –Say something!
At first, he did not say anything   he only smiled

When we were growing impatient, he said: —"very well"—
We said: we will not say "very well" anymore   they ordered us
                                                         not to—

He returned
He was weeping
He left
We know he is hiding under the ground

Now we are only burning
We are getting ready   we are burning
The ageless boy saying "very well"   had a strange tone
It was different from the tone of other people   even ours
A new question has come up:
—When will you fly on your own personal wings?—
We don't know
Perhaps the person who knew the answer to this question is
                                              hidden under the ground

We are burning
We are getting ready
We are burning

May 31, 1993

The Whirling Gaze
Whenever I move my hair from above my eyebrows
                                        you are sitting there
On the leaves, and in Darakeh   and the wind is blowing
                        and it is snowing   and   I am not there
Every day   I bought a flower   from the Amir Abad florist
                                            only one
But what eyes, haan! As if a couple of dates—
And I move my hair from above my eyebrows
                                        you are sitting there
I smoke a cigarette   you laugh   everyday   one stem
And I am reminded of the days when I was a little boy
And during the winters of Tabriz
Wearing my father's jacket as an overcoat
I would run along to school with my blue-eyed brother
                                through the tunnels of snow
And I wept   because they would say: This crazy kid always
                            has a tear drop in his green eyes
But what eyes, haan!   As if a couple of dates—
And with my blue-eyed brother   sometimes   we would go to
   watch the men being hung   at the Tabriz Clocktower Boulevard
And in the early morning   the snow fell slowly and settled on
      the heads of the men being hung   and, on their eyelids
The women   covered in veils   wept   the clock in the square
                                announced the world's time
I ran with my blue-eyed brother all the way to school
—This crazy kid   always has a tear drop in his green eyes
But what eyes, haan! As if a couple of dates—

In my life, the sun plays a minor role
Sadly, not being simple, has made me bitter
   otherwise, I would have told you and you would have laughed
When I feel like crying   I go in the back   I quickly peel an
                                onion so that others won't notice
Then I move my hair from above my eyebrows
                                        you are sitting there
I smoke a cigarette   you laugh   everyday a rose
                        three whole years   everyday
Night, is not my background   night is the hero of my movie
And the florist whose hair seems bluish violet under the light
                        told me one day: "why don't you give up?"
I said now I don't understand why being in love is human nature
                        and perhaps even beyond human nature
But   in my life, the sun   plays a minor role

This crazy kid   always has a tear drop in his green eyes—
Then I move my hair   You are sitting there

I would hand the flower to you and you would laugh
—By the way, my grandmother likes you   This is not your problem
                                             my problem is my mother—
And you would laugh
—But if you love me   Then why should your mother
                                             have a problem?—
—She is afraid of your eyes —
— t is eyes, not shoes for me to toss away   and then
     Buy a new pair of eyes from the market   and   wear them
—No, she says: "She's got to wear a new look, with no tears,"—
—I told you   in my life, the sun   plays a minor role
                                        and it does not dry the tears—

When I move my hair from above my eyebrows
                                             you are sitting there
Simin, Mehri, the flowers and your photographs laugh
And your hands tremble
Mehri and Simin's congratulations, and you?
                                             You bite your lips
—No! Those eyes don't match our family name
                                        They are rather strange
She must wear a new look, her look…—
Simin, who's bored, says, "Mehri, we shouldn't have brought flowers!"
Mehri says, "Flowers? Flowers? Flowers are useless! But take them!
And as for me?   I take the flowers from Simin in the street
And Mehri?   looks into my eyes   in silence   and then screams:
                    "There is nothing wrong with these eyes!"
And I sit down   and the Shah departs   and the revolution begins
Geography rises and invades the spirit of sleep
And the war, a burning bullet   remains   in the depths of
                                        the spirits of the youth
And Bolshevism   after a thousand distortions and chaos,
                                             is buried
—What did you say the child's name was, "Sohrab?" "Esfandiar?"
                                        And…how old?
—He's grown so much!—
Who said that all these years have gone by?—
I move my hair from above my eyebrows   you are sitting there
                                        and I am not there

And you ask, "What happened to your hair?"

–What was the child's name again?   And...how old?–
–Maybe a thousand years! I don't know
                                    What happened to your hair?–
Geography rises and invades the spirit of sleep
And your kids, where are they? What happened to your hair?–
And with my blue-eyed brother   sometimes   I would go
                                    to watch the men being hung
The women   covered in veils   wept
And I would run sometimes all the way to school through
                                    the snowy tunnels
And I would weep
–This crazy kid   always has a tear drop   in his green eyes–

I move my hair from above my eyebrows   You are sitting there
On the leaves, and in Darakeh   and the wind is blowing
                and it is snowing   and   I am not there
–But what eyes, haan!   as if a couple of dates
I smoke a cigarette   you laugh   everyday   a flower
–And where is your hair? –...I move it to the side–

June 17-19, 1993

Upside Down

I have always loved your black rose
But   I am stuck to myself   with the sharp nails that the
                            world has drilled into my soles
And I have slept your eyes too   when I am asleep
Now I am asleep
One day I was being threatened with the long, ornately carved
                         cane of a husband
When I was saved by his wife
The woman had read my poems
And the man knew about me through literary criticism of my poems

Without anything strange happening I jolt from my sleep
And I run into the pool   upside down   but which pool?
It seems that I am still running in my sleep

October 28, 1993

The Song

When John Lennon sings
With those kissing lips   placed on the song
I read a new style in those eyes of yours
Then I describe my dreams in the streets to people passing
                              by one after the other
Then I take flowers from the hands of the poor
And hang them on the shirts of world dictators
And I say, "Enough with the killing! Enough with the killing!"
And I liberate polite hands from the even politer knees at school
"Come out kids of the world, the poetry of the heavens has bestowed
                        itself upon you alone, instead of classes."
And I play music in all the garrisons of the world
And I play my musical instrument in all the garrisons of the world
With those kissing lips   placed on the song
When John Lennon sings

October 31, 1993

Now I See

–I don't know these birds at all
–I know   they were always there   they formed a great part of
the sense of your being

Like a woman who was produced inside you by another woman
whom you have known all your life

A woman was produced inside you
And this woman is different from the other women
you have known all your life

They were individuals
But the woman you have produced is not a collection of your
women, she's a producing woman

She is a spirit that if she oozes out of you and disappears in the
particles of the world, you will be destroyed

This woman, this producing woman, is the quality of her own birth
in a period of illuminated time

With a circular tongue

–But I don't know these birds at all
–This is the secret of clarity: You have kept the sea still so that
you can silence its roar

Let the sea roar, then you will recognize the flock of birds
When they fly from your imagination, as if they are flying beside
you

Thank you sound!   Thank you
You have given birth to the geography of the world's eye
Now   I see

Woman   thank you woman

November 10, 1993

Losing Consc…in Persian

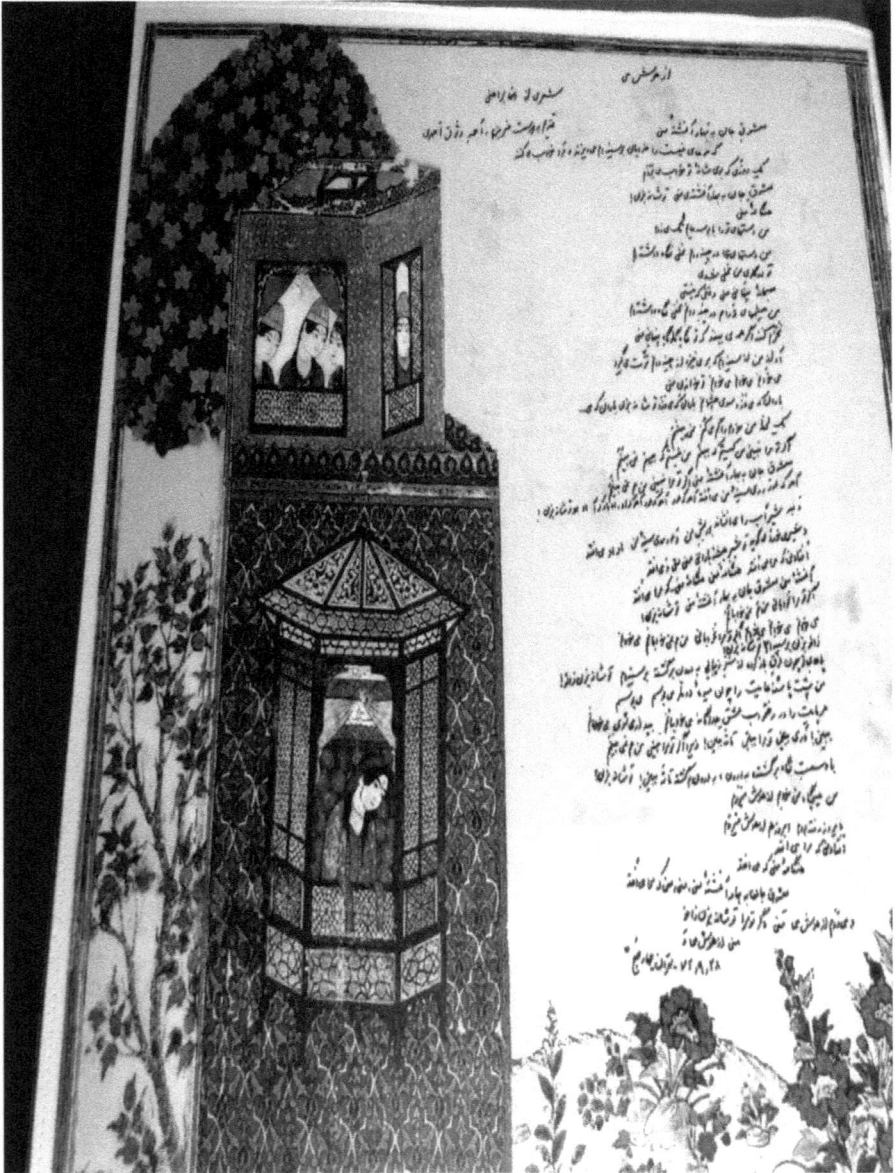

Losing Consc...

You are that spirit-immersed-in-spring of mine whose wet tresses
                    the Gods spread on my chest and put me to sleep!
You are that one day of mine when the scent of your shoulder puts
                                                    me to sleep!
You are that lover-immersed in-spring of mine   comb your hair!
You are my tumult
I pecked at your hands with my kisses
I hold your hands hidden in my pouch
You are hidden in my throat
You are my hidden breakfast when you are away
I have also kept your eyes hidden in my pouch
If they cut my throat, everyone will see you as the gaze of my
                                            hidden throat
My song rising from my chest, gains its strength from my pouch
I sing I sing I sing you are my singing
When it rains towards my eyes when it rains when it rains,
                        comb your hair! When it rains
For a moment I lose myself, I do not see myself
If you do not see me, who am I to see myself? Who am I to see
                        myself? I do not see myself
You are that spring-soaked lover of mine if you do not see me
                            I do not see myself
The deer that falls naked on my chest, the deer that naked
        the deer that naked, the deer that she, she, she, that she
                        she, she, comb your hair!
Then, she pours the water from the faucet onto my beard
                and naked on my chest   she she   falls
And she drinks milk   and tells me you are the lion of that rainy
                        forest of mine mine and she falls
A fall that falls me   you are that tumult of mine! You are that
                        tumult of mine –that falls me
You are that soaked-in-me, that spring-soaked lover of mine
                                comb your hair!
If you do not put me to sleep I will not put myself to sleep
I will sing I will sing I will sing if you do not put me to sleep I will
                not put myself to sleep   I will sing
I will raise my blood to my throat and sing, I will sing my blood
                                like a song
If they cut my throat, everyone will see that you are the gaze of my
                                hidden throat
If you do not see me, if you do not put me to sleep, I will not see
            myself either I will not put myself to sleep
Kneel on my chest! Comb your hair!

Your legs like a parted beauty turned inwards   onto my chest
                                        you comb and kneel
I kiss the backs of your heels like twin fruits   I kiss
I put each leg of yours to sleep in a separate bed of love
                              You wake up I put you back to sleep
See me! Yes see me to the end! Because if you do not see me
                              I cannot see myself either
See me with the breadth of a look turned inward, turned inward,
                    see me to the end!   you comb your hair!
If you do not put me to sleep, I will not put myself to sleep either,
     I do not see me   if you do not   now you comb and kneel!
I never sleep I simply faint
I fainted yesterday and I will faint today
A falling that befalls me you are my tumult that is falling,
        you are that spring-soaked lover of mine, mine, mine that
                                                befalls me
And I faint   mine   if you don't   you comb and kneel!   mine
                                          I faint   and

December 19, 1993

*I dedicate this poem to my friend and talented artist Ahmad Vosough
Ahmadi who grasps the heart of the matter.
                              R.B.

Fragmenting Into Fourteen New Pieces for The Dream, Wedding, and Death

1

With the red eye of an elephant that passes over a leaf
With the child in flames on the sacred river
At the station of death that only wants pieces of my body till
                                                          spring
Today, in the full courage of dawn   it rained
With the red eye of an elephant that passes over a leaf
With a forest that blows in the shape of wind instruments of fire
With mud-straw hands rising from India, the felicitous India
                                                          screaming
That I although very also with
And standing sleep so that the tempest   brings the hidden
                                    treasure to the surface of the water
And the door facing the window   I am tired
The coast withdraws from women's feet, all in the sea
                                    and the veils on the waves
Sometimes sharing the homes of whales in the hidden stables of
                                                          the waters
And they see the same no of perhaps   and one of them who
                                                jumps above me
I catch her to kiss her   she laughs and drowns
And the red eye of an elephant that passes over a leaf
Not without with   without with no   with without no
                              not without no   with   with

2

A hand as a window with lace veins of a song of you
                                        in the bird
Curtain drawn   on a face whose jasper nightcap also
And one day my father also here over the leaves and
                        naked without being in paradise
And the favorite fruit of my teeth   the moon   with
                                my bites from its face
And swarms of kisses that stranger
And a person with hardback eyes
And Euclidean gravure passing through sharp straits
                                        kiss me I said
Like the mast of nothing
Silently, the daf passed through the world's belly
                        and Egypt told the pyramids high
The willow tree that became bald on my chest
                                and hot as ice
If you don't kiss me now   I would not have been in the
                                        past either
The daf is standing on the summit of the highest of all
Hermes and Sadeghi have interwoven their improvised
                        fingers around this pyramid
And the moon   with my bites from its face

3

When he split the barrel in half with his sword
                                        I was asleep
—And a carriage with green horses stood beside us
                        on the second line of this poem—
I did not even wake up
In half of the barrel   some drunken people were
                                                watching me
And in the second half   was the orchestra beating itself
            eternally and madly like waves beating against cliffs
I was asleep   They were watching me
I did not wake up
I was the barrel split in two

4

When I was sieving the leaves of signs upon the dirt walls,
                                you told me, come kiss me
I had no lips
I returned   The half built wall went up my eyes
The sun was in a hurry   They were bringing you
At the window   The night was the name
                                            We were running
And the moon was turning around itself like a student
                                            learning a trade
I was with my brother   and you?   You were from a
                another millennium   and made love
                                in the language of parrots
We mounted the guests on our wings   and gave them a
                                    tour of their insides

5

My father died a hundred years ago
A hundred years from now I will be dead   my mother too
The world has changed   New York has become a hundred
                              times taller than the New York of our time
In Tabriz an ant is running like mad
And the tomb is always empty of poets
Now you say   No?
Under the nightcap   Shahriar's eyes recognize you

6

A man always drives me towards your scent
The season of doves in Chabahar is beautiful
Cramp is a twisted word that reaches the cradle in the
                                        marrow of the poem
So don't tell me that my city is being bullied by the sun
A woman does not
Have her want me   She doesn't personally want me

7

He said
Fetch the carafe of wine, the intoxication of silk,
                          the nine-fish carpet pattern under her feet
And the heavy saffron road running to the sky of the Kashani
                                              China plate

Pick them up
And bring them
—Who is it that says these things
—He is the person who has them brought
He is the meaning of having them brought

8
Only
A drum that is completely empty
And it's skin dry
And is blind too
Has a voice
Empty your lungs of air so that you can be a voice

9

Now that you are running me like mad day and night in the
                                   red light of the world
And have me brought in front of you   and then you have
                                          me taken away
So, what is left for me except your having me run, having me
                       brought, and having me taken away?
Nothing is left of me except the drum of my chest
Now that now now now that

10
Some say the obvious truth
Others the unspoken truth
I say the unspeakable truth
This:

11

I don't have to see you physically
I am so full of you, so full, that I am more like a beautiful joke
And in the evening the Vision Family came to ask for my hand
—And the suitor, young, upright, was holding flowers in his
                                        hand, when I said,
You have certainly seen my beard
And my mother took the flowers, put them in a vase, and said,
                            why kid a young man in love?
And she lowered her veil to her shoulders, and held up sherbet
                                and sweets, and smiled
I am so full of you so full
And the suitor screamed without any introductions, pen, carte
                                blanche, and mehr[10]
And he wept   I felt sorry for him because he was in love
And my mother explained that it's complicated because
                            her dowry is not ready
Her older brother has gone to India to fetch a parrot
                            and a Buddha
And the suitor gave a letter of recommendation from the
      French Counsel General traveling in Isfahan at the time
And he was wearing sunglasses and a helmet
And my younger sister watching through the curtains and
      giggling, was so adorable! She was still wearing a retainer
And the face of the suitor's father was a reflection of glasses
                            and eyebrows in the mirror
And he had fixed his eyes on my poor face
                            and he was horny
And I got up, and went into the mirror obliquely
And crossed over a thousand ports and lakes
And erected the sails of ships in your name
And went up a mast, and sat on top
And the scent of the sea came, the breeze carrying the
                      perfume of semen from whales in love
And the suitor came forward like the Caspian Sea holding
                  the coast and the jungle in his arms
And he wept   and shouted   like me
I am so full of you, so full, that I no longer need to see you
                                        physically
And he walked away
And my mother, seeing the stranger's eye veered away,

---

[10] Mehr - A gift from the groom to the bride at the time of marriage
in Islam

                                        took off her veil
And she started to dance on the deck of the ship
The rest of the people retreated

12

I take off descending on the rose the meaning of honey
And from Ilkhchi[11] to Ashooradeh[12] all the forests, the roads
                                    and coasts are off-limits
When you have rolled down the car windows saying how
                                        hot it is!
We sting, you scream, and the heedless sea pounds the coast
Thousands of honeycombs are taken by the waves
The feet of children and women sometimes taste like us
Sometimes my brothers emerge from the bellies of white fish
And our mothers are swallowing blood in the waters of the
                    Caspian asking where their children went
I'm a bird factory of production to consumption

When I fly I fall asleep   I even sleep when I sing
When I sit I either suck, sting or defecate
And the waters of the Caspian rose a hundred-thousand
                        honeycombs   just last night
Tonight is the thousandth millennium of bees
The sea is younger than our generation
Last night you got married   Now take it! I sting
                    The reward is sticky honey fingers

---

[11] Ilkhchi – City and capital of Ilkhchi District, in Osku County, East Azerbaijan Province, Iran
[12] Ashooradeh – Island off the Iranian coast on the Caspian Sea

13

Water, and enough are mixed
The flower drips on I don't know
So you are ready, and my birth is in the rain
It was before your birth that I fell in love with you
The flower drips
And I am either flung from the earth or fly
And my aunt sleeps from gunmetal and papyrus
From is not lovelier than with
Last night I ate in my sleep you have eaten me sleep
                                        the flower drips
Now for the last two days my corpse has been on the way
With enough water I had jumped over falling in love
The sparrow's ablution with hail on the power pole
The flower drips and the dove says Sunday, or Sunday
Together is not more lovable than from
In time won't even take me to Samarkand
Now get up and let's go it's time to go to sleep
We don't have time now, we'll go to sleep next year
And now mother gives birth to me

Now that we have no time we will be born next year
Six days are left to the end of the month of quails
And because the bat (shab pareh[13]) flew over the night steps,
                                        it was called, bat (shab pareh)
And copper and papyrus in the auntland of Samarkand's dawn
When the maid is being prepared so that Molavi and parrot
   and the merchant accompanied by the flute dance after prayer
Don't be afraid go ahead and dance
               I too will dance along with you   Now build me
I am made to be built

---

[13] Shab pareh – The Persian word for bat. The words translated into English would be night flight.

14

Have me brought
Have me put to sleep
Upon the silk road and beside a sparrow-sized opening
The lullaby of a nanny from your lips will take this young
     old man to an eternal snore or has me taken
Snoring is not in the realm of bears it is in the realm of humans
Your tresses are stuck in the threads of my throat
        You startle me from sleep
Now have me put to sleep again
Have me put to sleep under the sun
Have me put to sleep apart from the others
      Put me to sleep alone
Have me put to sleep by a sparrow hole
And have me put to sleep in the spring
Come from behind me and, look at me and worry about
      me day and night and then
Have me put to death with no concern Here Right here
I am not one to go to India or some other such place
      You bring India here Right here
And in the spring and by a sparrow hole
When the scent of your omelet takes over
And the pitcher of water gathers dew from the ice
Have me put to sleep yes here right here
I am leaving so that my leaving will be exactly my own
And it will be different from the departure of others
And now you part my spirit with your fingernails
I am in love with the head parted
And have the water poured on fresh earth I see
       I see you too
You are standing over there by the tree and you are
        glowing in tears
And this is my return towards the point of no return
Do not have me brought towards you any longer
Have me put to sleep
And lay the mirror upon me
The coma after death has so many details to analyze
Now I go from you, you are having me driven away
From every of, from every with, from every perhaps,
      you are having me driven away
And my twenty-four hours ended together at once
And now I am refreshing A hand of refreshing drives me
        towards nothing
The sound of moist refreshing repeat

Have me put to sleep
Have me brought
Like a poem I am at the crossroads of comparative birds
I have nothing toward song   nothing
A basket full of beauty at the opening of a sparrow hole
                                        and nothing
A pool of the spread of fresh in the broken glass
And now see how much my being lost has me bent
Having me brought toward me
I am smooth in the shape of lick numb   Having me brought
And my piece is being pressed into the others
                                        Even he has said this
…
And now whatever you are I am that   Have me put to sleep
And this blanket of mirror have it also sleep upon me
And suddenly the sound of the deliverer comes
                        and the deliverer is having me said
These things that I have said now the deliverer is having said
What the deliverer is saying
Who is it?   The one who is having me said?
Have me put to sleep   Have me brought and put to sleep
And now   my point of no return   complete
                        do not have me brought   I am asleep
Oh deliverer!   Oh delivering   Do not have me brought

November –December 1993

With Ahmad Shamlu
Influential poet of modern Persian poetry

Two shadows arms over shoulders in the dark it's you
                    and I left onstage and the hall is empty
And the children of weeping poke their heads from back stage
                    to see when the curtain will fall for good
Two blind singers nearing the green bench that was once a tree
And string instruments have been silent from the beginning
                                        of the night
That is all
You and I arm over shoulders in the dark
                    and when will the curtain fall for good?

November 26, 1993

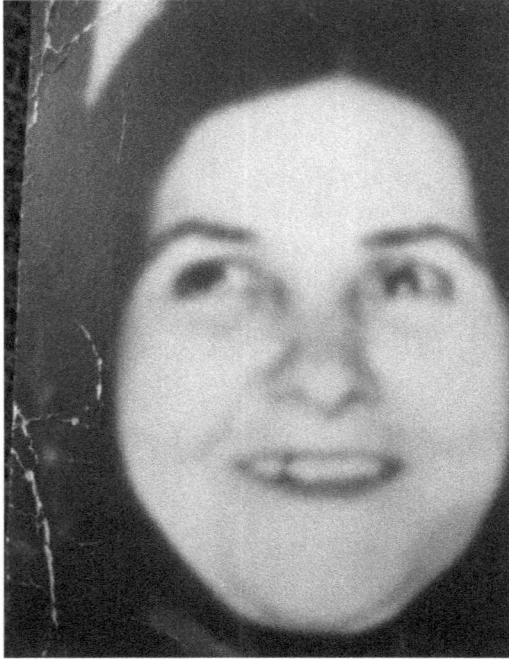

My beloved mother Zahra Soltan who told the best poems and stories although she was illiterate.

The Last Step
For my mother in the nursing home

When I die   Do not leave me among the tuberoses and
                                         the narcissi
Do not give me up   to the waters of the world
Do not entrust me   to the galaxies either
First pass me through the bangles of that oblique
                                         angled gaze
And take me up and beyond the broken stone steps towards
            the ancient trees whose shadows blow in the wind
Do not show me to anyone   not to my daughter, my
            brothers   my sister or my sons
What strange faces these people have sleeping on the beds
                                         of this room!
I am so tired!
Leave me on the last step   lay me down   return
                                         go back down
And take away the fruits, the flowers, and the dates
                              for they have no place here
Take me up and beyond   leave me on the last step
Your footsteps are the sound of fallen feathers from the wings
            of cranes in the season of the falling of the world's
                                         last leaves
The sound of your departure has ended   thank God!
I am so tired!   I need a long rest
Put me on the back of the desert spirit
And leave
And the next day if you want to come, come and
                                  bring a mirror
And watch the reflection of my sighs
See how this eighty-year-old young girl –a doll made
            of cloth –has fallen face down on the ground
Then   whirl me around myself
And hold me inside the bangles of that oblique
                                  angled gaze

Hold me and whirl me
Because I
Have never been

January 17, 1994

The World's Nursing Home

All those things that are being obliterated before my eyes
                            bring me closer to you
The geometric atmosphere of the leaves is in disarray
          How easily, the trees are all returning under the ground
The Earth, swallowed all its unevenness and became flat
Who said that the Earth was round?   It has a thousand
                        sides and angles in its deep shadows
The past, took over the Earth, in the shape of the lay of the
       pile of a threadbare nine-fish design carpet   folded it
       placed it behind the porter of wind, earth, and air, and
                                        took it away
And the city, the city withdraws in the form of a rumor from
                        the deep face of truth
Feverish time was given a footbath in the lake of moments
                            and hours
And the day is going not to return   and the moon
                        leaves so...and the night...
And the wind is hiding behind blowing   and light
                        behind sunrise
And the lock of sleep is in the red eyes of awakening
And the shoes, as soon as they are placed in pairs behind
                the door, no one will remain in the city
And the ships have reached the final phase of rushing towards
       the experience of returning to their preliminary particles
And invisible hands, are returning the steels of cars and the
                cast iron of trains back into the depths of the earth
And the horn of the rhinoceros of existence, returns behind
                the hill of existence in the form of a single cell
The world —a crumpled piece of paper —is stored in the
                        bottomless buckets of oblivion
And a concentrated fire, dumps the entire world into black
                        holes
The universe   an ice bullet
And   obliterated
And my small share of all this tumult of obliteration is the
                sound of a pure word: hail
The sound of that thirsty freshness   rejoicing   and style
    and the shape of a tub   gables and rain   and the plains
And several kilometers surrounding that room, there,
                the world   withdraws
And nothing remains except for that room and that too
                        withdraws
And that small wooden bed remains and that too—

                         as soon as you lie down   withdraws
And the moment I kiss you   and the moment the world
      becomes oblivious of itself   that kiss   too withdraws
And you laugh   in the shape of raindrops on glass, and,
    then, running, the end, and you disappear from my sight
All these things that disappear before my eyes
                                  bring me to you
The hail too   withdraws   and the nothing
                                 brings me to you
You too   withdraw: like perfume that ascends
          from itself into nothing, and is no more
And in the end
And now
I see you

February 17, 1994

Music

The piano is chopining a Chopin at the piano
                                                  and we do not hear
And we do not hear

                                   And we do not hear

And we do not hear

And we and we   and we   and we do not
Hear   and we   hear   and we do not

Hear   do not hear   and a Chopin behind a we do not hear
                          who Chopins
                                        that does

And
And
And we do not hear rrrrr…

Behind one   not Chopining   Chopin   not Chopining
                                   Cho   and Pin   Chopin
Do not Do not Do not Do not Do notCh   Chopining   and that
                 and that we hear   we do not heaeaeaearr

February 26, 1994

Note for the piece "Music":
This piece was written as a marriage of music and poetry. A transliteration of the poem in the Persian language is below so that the reader can get a sense of its rhythm.

Moosighi (Music)

Peeyano meeshopanad yek chopin be poshteh yek piyano
                                    va maa nemeeshenaveem
Va maa nemeeshenaveem

Va maa nemeeshenaveem

Va maa nemeeshenaveem

Va maa   Va maa   Va maa   Va maanemee
Shenavim   Va maa   shenaveem   vamaanemee

Shenaveem   nemeeshenaveem Va yek Chopin be
          poshteh yek nemeeshenaveem
                              ke meechopanad   ke mee

va
va
va maa nemeeshenaveemmmmmm

Be poshteh yek nemeeshopanad…..Chopin
      Nemeeshopanad   Cho   va   Pan   Chopin
Nemee   Nemee   Nemee   Nemee   Nemeesh
      Meeshopanad   va ke   ke meeshenaveem
                         Nemeeshenaveeeemm

The People in the Room

What kinds of people are these?
They walk behind the circles like dreams
There are birds with Esfarjan font wings that are sleeping
                                on the leaves of the world
With a deer gravure   from the forehead platform
And the sweet watery nip of first love on the earlobes
And underwater hair pouring among the rain of small fish
Like captivating trees in a place where no one is watching
What kinds of people are these that when you come to my
                                room and stay

They come too?

December 8, 1993

Burning

The star is not like you   you are not like the star
And the sky is not like you and you are not like the sky
The sadness that pours from you burns me
Spring is not like you and you are not like spring

Because you are standing in the breeze and burning
My barefoot beauty standing on the mat asleep
                                              and burning
The sadness that rains upon me from you...

And the battle between forest and magic that passes
                                              through you
And with your gaze my ring caught on fire

And nothing is like you   and no one is like you

My barefoot beauty standing on the mat asleep
                                  and burning
And beauty standing on the back of a tall deer, on fire with
            the joint of star and sea rushing and burning

Burns me   the grief that pours from you
And no dream is in the shape of your eyes none none

March 8, 1994

Rosebridge

I am a garden   and this shore   not you   she came to me
from the window   the world no   you   out of "the politics
of words?   No nothing   from a consciousness   and your
eyes when you got up from over the bridge   the wine shade
of your face   Yes?   Star   and this   when spring swore at
the city   Lost had made a pact with me on my breast to sleep
until the days of Adam and Eve   no   even not that   He
walks in the street and shouts the names of poets one by one
by heart   a shoulder-like fist   and   women   with white
and colorful faces   givveh (cotton shoe) and cat   deer, cat
and givveh   to walk from this side of the poem to the other
side of the bridge   to speak of walking and to walk speaking
and to walk not speaking   and this not saying and going not
to say and not going you flower   not like flower! Flower
To destroy the bridge after crossing, is the only bridge that
has been destroyed before crossing   alright   I am the
bridge   your destruction before and after crossing   you
flower and I? Rain upon you   whatever you are flower or
non-flower   I rain   not like rain   I even detest saying not
like rain not like a similarity   with no comparison   the
target is raining upon your flower or non-flower   let the
flowerless people pass   the flowerless is not non-flower
I the lion-keeper of the jungle, you with the lion I am roaring
in your jungle   and happy   the dew in the state of taking
shape upon a leaf   and the leaf of gathering upon the trees
of youth that run beside this river and nothing remains   we
go, no, not in our sleep!   That goes in the flower from
awakening to the other side of the bridge   Tear down the
bridge I so that I can cross over and now jump I jumped
my no saying also jumped now you go ahead   now you too
go ahead   no you too go ahead   this weight of the bridge
before being destroyed should be the dew of my raining upon
that flower raised the bridge and took off   who?
the one   now I say bridge and I do not get destroyed
and I fly from your shoulders   very well whatever you say
that   ok?   yes   the same   we walk this story we walk
the bridge we walk the flower now look!   I, become a
flower now jump   I become the bridge jump no I've
become the flower you jump the feather jumps from the
flower   dew twice   dew thrice   dew four times
dew a thousand times   the bridge slept   the bridge slept
on the precipice   we rebuild the bridge   it's easy   you
are on that side and I am on this side now we prepare the

precipice with this mutual caressing now, fly   no, fly later I
flew later say fly before I say   this kind of saying, is not
of the style of saying   this kind of saying is saying to find
the hidden meaning of things   it is a kind of caressing of
the hidden things   the bridge is being prepared by mutual
caressing   Prepare that hole so that the bridge can be built
upon it   yes   yes   stroke it with music   with the length
of your fingers caress it   prepare that hole now play tell
them to play the music of the preparation of the caressing of
the bridge   stop flying   pass   no, I will fly pass   no I
will fly pass pass pass   pass pass pass the pass   no I fly
no I fly no I fly   let the bridge pass   the dew a thousand
times over the flower   the bridge, has been revived
now color it with your kisses   wash the bridge with dew
and saliva and tears!   The bridge flares up   send the
children and the doves to fly above the fences so that they
can hang from the river   we walk   on the bridge
the flower saunters on the bridge   we walk the bridge
we walk the flower   the flower saunters the bridge saunters
the flower bridge towards bridge flower   say no more
bridge flower flower bridge   do not say anything
there's nothing else to say   I won't even say there's nothing
else to say   it makes no difference whether you destroy the
bridge behind you or ahead of you   destroy the bridge
very well   Did someone come?   I plant a flower above
your ear in the garden tresses   I wash you with dew, saliva,
and tears   and I cross the precipice,   and the bridge in my
pocket,   the bridge in   and the children and doves are
hanging above the bridgeless river   and the bridge hidden
from your view   and now go back   and start the circle from
the beginning   I am a garden   and this shore   not you
she came to me from the window   the world no   You

June 14, 1993

The Hidden Speaker

Are you depressed that you have so scattered your hair on
                                        my chest?
Do you not know that I go blind when you see me?
Are you so depressed?
I am beating you below your chest. Prepare your internal
                                        ears to hear me
I am beating you with my fists, with my heart, with this black
                                        Are you depressed?

I held your ears firmly so that you could not hear
        We were in the garden   I was screaming so that you
                                                could not hear
My world war with you started from my chest   My beginning
                always started from the end or the middle
                                        Are you depressed?

I was beating you with my ears so that you wouldn't hear that
                                you were hearing me

We were in the garden   But which garden?
Of the description of the garden only a pair of blossoms
                        of blood are still terrifying in my mind
I was screaming so that you could not hear me
You told me you ate snakes, hence the evil glow in your eyes
I told you I go blind whenever you see me
Are you depressed?   To this degree?

A bridal tray honoring vision and another honoring
                                        blindness
We were in the garden I was going blind   You were
                        seeing me and I was going blind
It was absolute darkness around us
I was beating you behind your skin I was beating you inside
                your spine I was beating you non-stop
From that hidden prenatal universe of mine, from the chest,
under the chest, I was screaming and beating you mercilessly
Are you so depressed?
You told me you wished this night had never happened
I told you I am always with you on the last night
                        Come closer   Closer!
Closer than this? I am hidden beneath your chest cavity
                I am beating you   closer than this?
Yes closer!

That Eastern priest of double-genders invaded us
We were being combined   Closer! Closer than this?

My world war against you started from my chest, beneath
                                        my chest

There were no ruins between you and I and the entire universe
The ruins started later
You scattered your hair on my chest –Are you so depressed?

The scribe turned into the book the written text was
                                        concealed in my writing
I was beating you with my book and you were beating me
          with my writing   we hid   Are you depressed?

I am dog-spirited   you are the human
You are Joseph, I am the odor of your shirt, I am your wolf
No! I am Joseph, you are my shirt, Am I Canaan?
                                        You are Canaan
We hid   Are you depressed?   To this degree?
When we passed through each other like a river
                    What was left?   Are you depressed?
My howls awakened East and West regions alike and
                    remained awake   I am dog-spirited
Come closer   Come closer   Closer than this?

I was holding your ears firmly so that you could not hear
     We were in the garden   I was shouting so that you
                                        would not hear

And I was going blind   I was screaming so that you
                                        would not hear
Of the description of the garden only a pair of blood
                    blooms are still shivering in my memory
The woman's hair poured from the beams of the stage
                                        ceiling
And the curtain fell upon her suspended face
Rushed photos of a pair of blood blooms   Closer than this?
All East and West regions were kept awake by my howls

We were in the garden   But which one?
In the garden of finding?   No!
In the suspended gardens of Babel or China?   No!
In the garden in the bedroom in Gonieh when my wife

was shouting from behind the door and I would say,
                              "One moment! One moment!"
No   it wasn't there   A Turkish Oedipus?   No!
                    These things do not appear on the stage
I was beating you below your chest, beating you with my
      fists, beating you with my heart beating you fearlessly
Are you depressed?
It wasn't there   Where were we?   Certainly in a garden
                                        But which one?
Breathe with me and blow your breath into my chest
      I had blown before   Blow now   Is that you?
                                        Yes it is I

It was pitch black everywhere   But which garden?
They were weaving the carpet of a garden on my chest
      the fingers of your hair invisible they were screaming
                                        and weaving

Oh displaced from me   Gone to a different century than
      mine   from another atmosphere than mine
                              in another galaxy than mine!
Are you depressed?   Are you so depressed?

A Turkish Oedipus who plucked his eyes behind the scene
                              under the sun?   No!
The ashes spread on the stone stage?
The snore of an old horse reaching our ears from behind
                                        the stone stage?

The corpse hanging by the hair from the ceiling beam?
The crescent snake passing the roof of the soul?
A blind man sitting on the back of an old horse riding on

Closer than this?
A bridal tray honoring vision and another honoring
                                        blindness
As I said
I am hidden under your chest   I am beating you with
                                        my fist
I am beating you with this black   Are you so
                                        depressed?
Is that you?   Yes, it is I

June 24, 1993

I Am Addressing You Beautiful Lady Iraneh

You are not aware of the agony I have suffered you are not aware
                                                                beautiful lady

Now I leave everything to you although I have no home here
                                                                no home there
I do not have a head so that you can bring me a bucket
I am addressing you beautiful Lady Iraneh!

Whether you comb or do not comb all that hair, whether you
                                                part it or not, I am that part
Look at the back of your head in the mirror, beneath the ground in
                                        the mirror I am with you beautiful lady
Even if the face remains back there for a thousand years I am still
                                                behind that curtain with you
Whether you thrust the crown of your hair across continents
                                                I am there naked with you
Without you I am a beggar, a beggar of the world's streets
I am addressing you beautiful Lady Iraneh!

I am speaking these words from the place where the breast touches the
                                                                waist
I am with you from the place where the wetness of dewdrops water the
                                                                hairs of dreams
I am speaking with you of the place where the ear and the nipple sit on
                                                                the moon
I am speaking with you of the place where we are parallel only a kiss
                                                                apart then nothing
The eye you have one, now make it two, parallel, yes parallel
I cannot dream of you I cannot sleep and therefore without sleep I
                                                                cannot dream
I am addressing you beautiful Lady Iraneh!

If you comb your curls of hair upon my chest I won't tell myself I won't
                                                        tell myself that I am lost!
There is no thought for me to think I think about nothing so that I can
                                                        say it correctly I am lost!
I won't call the earth to the cows and the clouds to the doves
I won't call the clouds to the moths, owls, and the hoopoes

Thinking of nothing I won't write poetry with open eyes, I won't call the
                                        moon trapezoid
I won't say anything I won't that I am lost!
If one's knees aren't woman
If the waist is not saffron and woman, I won't say anything
I hate geometric shapes so much, where is my shoulder that was in the
                                        open beautiful lady?
I am addressing you beautiful Lady Iraneh!

If sadness doesn't wander then wounded forever
If the face cannot face the sea
If the morning cannot be bloody, all those heads, all those chests, are
                                        not mine bring me a bucket

When the head goes to the woods and the leaves to the dead
The face cannot face the sea
Now that we are congratulated with the dagger of exile and have a place
            lost in my heated throat where I am lost and blood spills
I was already your victim, why did you turn me into a victim again
                                        beautiful lady
I am addressing you beautiful Lady Iraneh!

Should the ear become so small that the water should subside and dawn
            know again like two eyes in the night beautiful lady
I won't say anything so that she will know
I am thinking of nothing so that I will whistle
You heard the comb disturbing my hair
My spirit is in turmoil licking the inside of your mouth when the glass
                                        broke
Do you not remember how I threw my words up to the sky? How I
                        placed the underworld over my head
Seeing your eyes behind the shoulder back to the sea and
                        the carpet expressing so many patterns of joy
So do it! Ah! Do it again! Enable yourself to do it again!
Under the ground above all scent crying with kisses words
                                I do not understand
So enable me because nothingness is moving me towards
                                        thoughtlessness
The garden changed the morning bird sang beautiful lady
I am addressing you beautiful Lady Iraneh!

This habit of looking behind me, beautiful lady!
Never escapes my mind
This habit of drawing curtains from the window
Seeing them, them, them their daggers God's grave, how does this
                    how does this never escape my mind
This habit of these shrill screams never end so that I can give you
                                        my head
After all was I the one who died these young deaths
Was I the one who shed this blood? A forest of wild animals
                        surrounded in the eyes of a gazelle's dream
Was it I?
This habit of saying these thoughts in the manner of not telling
Again how? That nothing to never that earth to sun and I to woman
                                    and woman standing there
I am addressing you beautiful Lady Iraneh!

I made myself more lovable on the inside so that you could return
                                so that love would return
I disappeared like the sea foam so that asleep I could sing
Like a whale the color of a hidden absent
The moon swimming on parts of her foamed buttocks without her
                                        knowing
May the fish come in the shape of your eye
Saying this beautiful death at the pinnacle of the deepest part of the
                                        universe
Mystery is that index finger upon the panting circular flesh
I am not going to write that I am dead, that you turned me into yourself
                            and drink well in the underworld
I am not going to write beautiful lady!
I am addressing you beautiful Lady Iraneh!

These pupils see the sea, the rain, the underworld three
These pupils see the sea
These pupils see the rain
These pupils see the underworld
How can they see underworld three?

Look far like the wind, like the bird and woman
I am not going to write that I am going to die
I am not going to write again that I am in that underworld
I will not write that this vast place pristine to infinity can be tiring
Your puzzled face and the blood in your look
The crooked laughter, the smallness of lips, lemon rinds and fingernails
                                    fingers so pure

Becoming a child like the wings of a bird
The hidden tears in the underworld of three you are saying, so what can
                                                  I do from under here
The moment's bright intelligence, the moment of departure
What can I do without you, what can I say, and that beautiful lady
Saying that I will do whatever you tell me
Not allowing the forms of separation into the underworld
Wanting from the bottom
He to you, I with you, and all of us facing you to the end
Entering the river through the underworld channel and kissing three
Opening the eyes in your underworld waters your back to the sun
                                                  and the moon sleeping
Seeing those lemon rinds and pure fingernails of fingers
Holding the spirit between the teeth and passing through the liver of
                                                                love
And then to see a door ajar, and to go through
Sleeping and dying in the eyes that take bloody pieces of the eyelids
                                    crying Oh my homeland!
A dagger of love that pierced through the only single look that
                          remained with me, woman! Oh my homeland!
So what should I do with such bitten lips, bloody gum, amidst stars,
                                    in the underworld! Woman!
Saying that bloody word of love that only us, –so what should I do?
          to say or to hear it and to know that we have the power
He with you, I with you, and all of us facing you to the end
The spelling out of shiny lullaby dewdrops and the depths of shiny
                                                           crevices
To deliver the spirit to the emptiness of no thought
What can I do without you the weight of this what can I do without you
                              what can I do beautiful lady?
I am addressing you beautiful Lady Iraneh!

During the day when I am addicted to your opium, at night when you
          are addicted to mine, do not leave me behind because I will run
                                                  from myself
Lips murmuring the eyes in the underworld again
At night I turned you to myself, and during the day you turned me to
          yours and I turned them to myself now from the first Spring
Now enable yourself! Now enable yourself again! You who turned
                          this dear earth into turning into Spring
On Fridays between the week of thighs on top of I will say on top, I
                              am on top beautiful Lady
No memory of yours comes to mind, come yourself, come naked, make
                    me think of nothing, with you beside me

I am addressing you…
You are not aware of the agony I have suffered you are not aware
                                               beautiful lady!
I am addressing you beautiful Lady Iraneh!

Do not leave me behind because I will run from myself to the
                         underworld, oh homeland! Woman!

July 1997

الگا

احرٍ که لطیفٌ با تو بودن
جمعیت مدید است بر ایوان
وقتی که به بیشه‌های خرّم‌اند
آمد پر است چشم او چران
احرٍ لطیف با تو بودن
گلی‌ست
در چشم تو گنجینه‌ی او ریسه

نوشته توسط رضا براهنی، تهران بستر، در سرزمین در چنین مه آمریکا
بران انگار عزیز، دفتری برام یادگار

دکتر رضا براهنی
ششم دسامبر ۲۰۱۵
تهران

The Gentleness of Being with You

Aleca!
The gentleness of being with you
Is the sum of a flock of swallows on a veranda
A deer standing still, eyes awestruck
      in the persimmon groves
The gentleness of being with you
Is a treasure
Its roadmap resting in your eyes

December 6, 2015

Selected English Poems

Requiem for Allen Ginsberg

Flesh of heart cutting itself on the single
lip of that dagger of tranquility now
I, Reza Baraheni, mourn the poet Allen Ginsberg
mourn now in foreign English   darkness
of eighteen years away from you I mourn wasted
in the shiftlessness of swampy dungeons of
Godless religions I mourn

Generations disemboweled in Howl   pain
contrasted to the saccharine smile of politicians
mother of poets dug out in "Kaddish"
caged woman in all men   Tibetan Buddhas
of solid chests of young boys   urethras merging
into gutters of prostate   sizzling come
guzzled down in half-scared throats   then
shining of the moon on the single lip
of that dagger of tranquility now   I mourn
poet Allen Ginsberg I mourn

Blind old horse of a head held frozen upwards
eyes glued to darkness   listened to the
subterranean earthquake of rising words   took off
suddenly, not out into the open fields but over his craggy
cheeks with abrupt flow of tears   Borges   listening
to lines of Hafez read to him by me at your behest
sacred calligraphy of blind tears   and that night
in New York you had no beard on your
face   and the two of us watching him in silence
two birds watching an old bird in silence

We took each other's arms   the only arms poets
and other slaves of words could take   fought the only holy
war of the spirit   releasing other slaves of words
bastard regimes only changed hands   we moved from
one cell to another   each in his cell   Eliot's
tired voice in images of Dante's *Hell* and I've
lived two hells   no purgatory   no paradise
and believe me Allen, I am unprepared for a third

Burnt out candle of words sunk in history reference
forced you to lose some of your poems to politics
Vietnam, good cause, hopes badly placed
but great poems came when you were
in a hurry   as if in danger of silencing them
the will to desire thrust your hybrid
voice into the sphincters of heteroglossia
you became the *other*   against others
yours were haste poems of catch
and hatch   black and white wedding of total strangers
on the sudden bench of old train stations
your words passed through the thorn-field of
your pained throat   almost lipless   even mouthless
the words sang by themselves   but only *almost*
if I mourn Allen Ginsberg I mourn the
distance between that *almost* and the absent *perfectly*
the great and deepened *lack*
the lack that is the poet Allen Ginsberg I mourn

April 16, 1997

Exile Poem of the Gallery

In the *Portrait of Apollinaire*
one eye of the poet is closed like Odin's,
the double chin is lifted to one side of the face
and the countenance is a moon blinded by its revolution
Yet this
is not what the Persian poet sees with both eyes
Chagall has put
Over Vitebsk between the three eyes of the two poets
The year is
1914, when the 19th century ended and human flight began
in Vitebsk

In Rodin's *Adam*, the absence of divine clay hurts the hands
of prehistory   It is black and heavy   God molding it
in the Age of Iron, with no touch of irony   Instead,
you see the organic unity of Rilke's sonnet to Orpheus
A pity that Orpheus is not there with Rodin   *Adam*
would have been replaced by Eurydice, the woman in ashes
waving her soft hand, disappearing   Rilke, the apprentice,
 too timid to suggest it to the master, had to go to the
steppes of Pasternak's Russia and Chagall's Vitebsk.

"Kiss my lips. She did."[14]   Whenever I see these words,
I run, then I fly, not freely, that is for Chagall, but
in a plane, to look down and see as Picasso
did the canvas, and Gertrude suggested that we should see
all his paintings as if looking down from a plane, since the
"war was the composition of cubism."   Picasso inherits
the earth from the sky, dividing and blending frontiers
And Blake had said: "To create a little flower is a labor of ages."
    This time, Eurydice
descends from the sky to lay her face on the double-mooned
face of the poet in the Gallery's Picasso "Kiss my lips over and
over and over again she did."[15]

But I am not talking of this flight, and this 1914.

First, I have to walk to the biggest hall to wake up my son
sleeping under the legs of the draped female colossus,
a Henry Moore

---

[14] From the poetry of Gertrude Stein
[15] From the poetry of Gertrude Stein

"I have feathers/Gentle fishes."[16]   And Aba Gertrude is my
mother's title
in heaven   Where I am watching a few Picassos in the
Art Gallery of Ontario   "In the midst of our happiness
we were very pleased."

He sleeps there, the childhood of a long-haired deity
All around him children re-collapse and re-collect their
turbulent games, with parents and instructors
frenzied to educate them in the ways of stone and flesh
My son's dream is an education   Gallery objects wash him
in ether   He has a half-open, half-kissed mouth,
his mind gallery crowded with softwares of arcane material.
And stone is a stone is a stone in Mr. Moore   Here it is,
copious,
but not to be copied   And the game goes on Herculean
arms are needed to unhinge the stones, reclining on their
elbows, knees and buttocks   Only a god could give you
a tour of these Moores in the Gallery, by lifting them all
on the tips of his fingers and nursing them by his lips
Male stones of stability cast
in female figures of needless heaviness
each poised, regular or irregular, like a sterile
island of desire, thirsting for passions of hammering rain
Round cavities, peopled by smooth half-shoulders and
half-backs,
and single-fingered fists of female nipples, left untouched after
the first touch of their master mason   Silent homes
of human members, each in search of an antediluvian desert
to live happily ever after with the rush of the sand
and the push of the wind   The gigantic magic of curved
slabs rising musically to end in upturned faces
And how hard to say:
"I have feathers/Gentle fishes," in this hall   Carry them all
into open air   The zoo needs a breath of the forest.
"I am waiting here...I'm tired of standing --- Let us fly together"
Chagall must have said these words
watching the uplifted toes of 19th century ballerinas in the
next hall
"Ton visage écarlate ton biplan transformable en hydroplan."[17]
Apollinaire must have seen it in Au-dessus de la ville, lovers

---

[16] From a poem by Marc Chagall
[17] From a poem by Apollinaire on a painting by Marc Chagall

flying freely over the city in colors, the spine of the woman
openly made pregnant by her own buttocks   Two arms and
only three elegant shoes   But they are flying and who cares?
I have also seen his La promenade, the horizontal beauty in
                                                    the air.
The lonely Chagall in the Art Gallery of Ontario has a date
I have gone through valleys of bronze and marble, and all
pastures of faces and lines and eyes and hips, and I have
noticed this: the epitome of my empathy
                              This: Over Vitebsk, 1914
The crisis reflected in flight of the doomed and the damned
The borders, as always, are closed
the wars are beginning, the pages of exile
are opening before your very nose   And Chagall
places my hat on the old man's head, hands him the cane of
                                        Oedipus
throws a beggar's sack on the man's bent shoulder
And makes him walk in space, over the city of Vitebsk
in Gogol's Overcoat. We have to change the faces and
figures of all coins all the moneys   And change all the flags
There remain only three things: the epitomes of our empathy:
the "Sketch for Over Vitebsk," 1914; "Study for Over Vitebsk"
                              and Over Vitebsk,
1914. Three things in all three of them: the man in flight;
the schizophrenic gulf under him; and the city split in half:
the non-place of exile century
No one has a country.
And the lonely Chagall in the Gallery keeps the exiled poet
                                        focused,
changing the figures, the notes and the flags
and even languages
and Chagall inherits the sky as country
and the sky as language
and the poet looms over the precipice
with a dagger thrust in his throat
with his tongue caught between his teeth
performing the sacred duty
of writing this very poem of exile.

March-April, 1999
Toronto, Canada
Published in Making Meaning, Toronto Art Gallery of
Ontario, 2000

Women Shot at Childbirth

Nations outliving executioners are
free   maybe

Only in the next room they're
showing a Nazi movie of shootings in Warsaw

Are free executioners outliving
nations   for sure

But movies are not made only of shooting
generally the abstract smile of a woman
a kiss of birds   a neat zest
a field powdered by mist   a cap   the uniform
follows   galloping of horses   whistlings
of the moon   wheels   tired wheels in
the mud   a flawless rape of innocence

Not the one in the next room
a movie for ears   not eyes
shootings in Warsaw

Is it a room? A movie? Warsaw?
1981 that begins at nine at night
and runs to daybreak

How my life depends on the head of odors
inside me   a girl   I want a girl

Moves under fingers of salted blindfolded night through every night

1981

Death of a Greek Woman in Seattle
For my first wife upon her death in 1997

1
Eyes
eyes watching exile at windows of carcinoma
a minute before the death of desire   Helen of Thessalonica,
rained upon, you will be from now
to the day of rising in dust rags or not rising at all
in Seattle, U.S.A.
Helen of Thessalonica

Devouring death at the irritant uterus   Hades rising
from powdered ankles, past ghost knees up devastated
thighs inviting pursed lips from your hurt mind when being
                                                            washed
and cadaver curvatures of pelvis and broken hips   past
                                                            withered,
in-closed vagina down   down where one doesn't know
                                              past former
Constantinoples of breasts facing the forest beyond in the
                                              thoughtless rain
and irradiating Bosporus eyes awaiting
the absurdity of no time   visiting on sawdust heels
                                                    palaces
torn down in other continents of mind   (those arcane
                                              galaxies of
dismembered goddesses)
mind that no longer minds
raining   raining yourself into that Orthodox hell of a hole
In Seattle, U.S.A.
Helen of Thessalonica

Eyes
eyes watching the eleventh minute film of a new Herodotus
covering the distance of pages between my Athens, your
                                                    Persepolis
Breasts
four thundering swords of breasts clashing in the dark
raining into you lakes of my essence
raising above you boats of my Caspian clouds
Flying   flying

flying arms and shoulders and birds and kicks and wings
an Istanbul of Chagalls painting what?　Four millennia of
                         statues
almost untarnished standing above tombs
withdrawn into underground chimera　Sixty ravens sitting
                         heavily
on electric wires of your age　Tell me
Eyes watching exile at windows of carcinoma　not seeing
not seeing anything in the world, but painting
as blind painters of the Louvre paint with seeing ears
the world beyond me
in Seattle, U.S.A.
Helen of Thessalonica

2
Carrying and caring
caring and carrying the carcass of Dionysus at my back
to the Ganges where it originally belonged
washing the limbs one by one　Kissing
kissing the ankles, the lingam, the knees
the knees, the shoulders and the ticklish eyelashes
of the wide-open eyes　kissing and weeping
and wiping away the heavy dust under the skin
the liminal Dionysus, the truncated one　the hybrid beauty
kissing and caring, because only caring I know how to care
going back　taking him back to the original river
And his women I know will follow him to the pyre
burning and burning alive　And were you one of them
In Seattle, U.S.A.
Helen of Thessalonica?

A precipitous Dardanelles of distorted words
in Greek, Turkish, Persian and English forests
pouring into your blocking straits of mind　Forgetting
your Dionysus of fleshy fingers, honey eyes and sensual lips
and the labyrinth of ears brimming with your *khamisa to*
                         munimou
rain pouring down and down out the window in Seattle
And your eyes watching the fish rising to touch your fingers
in the heat in the sun in Bosporus,
the Islands, or perhaps in Greece?　And there were two
                         ranges
of islands, one in Greece and the other in Istanbul,

and the ship took us to the second of these   Cavafy
coming through, as Auden had said,
even in the bad translation in English, but here, thanks
to your teeth, the tip of your tongue, the Greek mouth
and Durrell's remarks in the Quartets
(And Cavafy was a devil
watching the young sailors in Alexandria sauntering
by the burnt down Borgesian library, and picking the best
                                                  one
for his night collection of thighs and memory   Keeping
                                    the window open
touching the roots of the hair
entering regally the classic body   Writing the poem an
                                        hour later
in the mask of the hazel eyes of the sailor
listening to the bouzouki from the square, smoking an
                                        Egyptian pipe
breaking almonds with gay fingers
drinking wine to the health of passing Coptic harlots)
                        and you carrying yourself
to the last gasp of a dream
through the window in rain, because there are
no barbarians any longer, who would have been a
                                        solution
There you are once more
in the carriage on the hills with the sea rising to meet
                                    your eyes
in the arms of the barbarous poet, dreaming that this was
                                    the right profile
for the watch hanging from his chain   This was going to
                                        turn around
many times and many years   until it survived
in the rented house of words and turned into a poem
as many years later as possible in the last gasp of the
                                        woman
in Seattle, U.S.A.
Helen of Thessalonica

3
Be sure that I will take the carcass of Dionysus out of
                                        Greece,
out of Euripides, out of Holderlin and Nietzsche,
set him up on the pyre of the mother by Ganges
and watch him burn to ashes

I won't let anyone near the ashes
I won't sing as Seferis sang of broken images
(in my case it is broken languages)
or as Ritsos[18] sang of rifles pointed at the temples of
                                        young poets
although I may have shared a lover and a few ideas
                                        with him
No, I won't let anyone near the ashes
They are my ashes   They are you.
Hidden in each other we will withdraw from the earth
leaving it to the loneliness of its rocks, waves and
                                        peoples
forgetting the joke of tragedies played for our names
and hide, hide forever from everyone
as you are hiding now
in your ashes
in Seattle, U.S.A.
Helen of Thessalonica

4
Standing in the street now with tambourines played
to honour Queen Elizabeth and the Shah of Iran
                            the bared bayonet
on the rifle held across the itching tip of my nose
(but what could be more tangential than the making
                                        of history
when a man stood there watching
and thinking only of you Lija-mu?)
                            how could I know
that you had taken the train to Ankara, the bus to
                            Erzurum,
the car to Tehran, with a female Alexander on your lap,
clinging to the subconscious butterfly, a notion of India?
(the trip the three of us were to take only in our minds;
by the way, were you breast-feeding still,
with the butterfly there forever?)
then standing for seven more years in the streets
in a completely unknown city, with unknown languages
not wanting to know that the strangeness of words
was another version of your own mind in exile

---

[18] Yiannis Ritsos – (Greek: Γιάννης Ρίτσος; 1 May 1909 – 11
November 1990) was a Greek poet and communist and an
active member of the Greek Resistance during World War II.

thinking always of the rocks, the bouzouki, the past
                                        that hurt
and the future that had to bring in the past as it had been
otherwise it would be no future   Tending to the
                                        wounded bones
of a poet in need of your hands, and in need of what else?
Both of you in exile, two samples of two different species
sticking together as foreigners in a strange land,
a mirage of faces, the dogged begging of addicts, the
                                        innocent sneer of students,
the poverty of hands and faces all thrown into the network
of ruthlessly rundown offices, dilapidated traditions
of an overworked nationalism of merchants, grocers, and
                                        bureaucrats,
and users of beautiful words, as always on the wrong
                                        occasions
and you, detesting all of them, resisting from turning into
                                        one of them,
but not even wanting to go away
something that kept you obstinately there for seven years
now lying in your ashes somewhere else
(and what a destiny!)
in Seattle, U.S.A.
Helen of Thessalonica

5
Then the lover turned into a hearsay,
a euphemism for exile, the reality being there
always at a distance from where you were, a combination of
love and hatred, another euphemism for exile,
                                        as if once mentioned
it could subvert the universe of honour
a feeling that you are not supposed to have for your mother
but you certainly could have for the father.   And you start
                                        all over again
to give birth to the mother, in exile, so that this here at
                                        Massey,
in Toronto, where I am, and you there in Seattle
where you languish in your ashes, poorly mourned,
will have a language.   For, a mother has to be born,
                                        not a son,
not a father, not even a daughter, although she could be
                                        a mother later,
a mother has to be born. In a language she could not

have heard of;
in this kind of English that I write; the universal hearsay
                              of English;
a rumour spread for all over the world to see and fathom,
the phantom of a mother; not a foster-mother, no; that is
                              not giving birth
but a mother gathering back into her womb
languages that had been born in spite of her,
gathering back into a stomach that smashes everything
                              into smithereens
and giving birth to the hearsay, which is the language of
                              exile,
the universal, the pre of all pres and the post of all posts,
and the now of all nows
climbing Mount Etna as your bald-headed Empedocles
                              did
with infernal fumes rushing, rushing into his brains,
                              cursing
Cursing Socrates and Plato of a century later
for depriving gods of ambrosia
and deporting singing women to the lands of a dark
                              genesis amnesia,
an Alzheimer's thunderbolt that struck the lunar female
                              mute,
cursing and falling, falling and cursing
into the arms of a burning deep past
while I sit here as Holderlin sat on the steps of the
                              carpenter's house
watching him saw the tree for wood for his coffin,
and wet the nails with his lips
and forgetting and smiling   Just as I am forgetting
                              and smiling
at your eyes in the burning deep past
dead in exile
in Seattle, U.S.A.
Helen of Thessalonica.

February, 2001
Toronto, Canada

The Cross Moon

The grand exile of love's emirs
    that eclipsed moon
        that pure, gold-shining, shining moonlight
           hasn't he come back yet?
             that moon in a prison
                that cross moon
                    hasn't he come back yet?

We, eyes inflamed with weeping,
    We, eyes washed in this jungle, the eyelashes of the
        jungle, the jungle of eyelashes -
           eyelashes washed,
                roots planted deep in blood,
                  we sit here, sit
                        with eyes washed,
                          in blood washed

Hasn't he come back yet,
    the beloved, eclipsed,
        the grand exile of love's emirs
           the shining, pure, gold-shining
                -moonlight –
                  that cross darling
                    hasn't he come back yet?

September 4, 2002

The Key

"This is my morning, my day is breaking: rise now, rise, thou
                                                            great noon!"
Nietzsche, *Thus Spoke Zarathustra*

1

It was sweating and swelling in my palm
the key, I mean, when the leaves fall off in the cold rain
back in the yards, on the short walls everywhere, and over
                                                            my bags
on this side of the wall; and my shoes and clothes soaked
                                                in tears and blood
but it was the bloody memories that hurt
the sky, as always, in its tragic mood   And I had to be
                                                tough—
with parents, brothers and sisters, and so many friends
buried in unknown graves, miles and miles apart
                                                and one day,
in another life perhaps, I would go once more to find them
and lay the stones on their graves, giving them new names
                                                and new dates
Yet I knew, I knew that I was lying to myself to get myself
                                                going   I locked
the door to the ancient castle in ruins, to virgin deserts
hidden in the night, cemeteries shivering in the fog in the
                                                dawn,
with the hands of the dead sticking out
supplicant for a word of prayer in this hour of hasty
                                                departure
Oh, the hell with the past—the traitor—
with unsheathed daggers of bloody memories
held high in the hands of all those hooligans
And I hurled the key back into the yards of the Eastern
                                                zone
"Take it! It's yours, for good!" And walked past several
                                                religions,
a dozen histories, thousands of cities, continents of
                                                mouths
frozen in passion and fear   walked past lovers, the
                                                heartaches,
memories of epileptic bodies beneath and above me,
                                                overheated
perfumes of holes, chaotic words of incestuous desire and
                                                treason, and time,

time spent thinking in hurt and pleasure about those faces
                                        and arms
and thighs; illicit, unwritten documents of imagined
                                        love-scenes,
so close to the memories of the body; and walked past
                                        myself, leaving
even that myself behind: "Take it! It's yours, for good!"
                                        and deprived the
drama of the audience it never deserved, burning all
                                        reference and keeping
only this tattered coat of words; these feathers of birds,
                                        long tongues
of total strangers for more than half a century.
Oh the hell with even the entire century!
What difference does it make! All new countries
are populated by bastards, and you are one of them
Change your name, your parents, your children, your
                                        codes!
Do not ever go back, walk towards the future, and you
                                        are the total stranger,
and so is everyone   Classic notion of scavenger gulls
in the morning of Guelph, Ontario that carried the
                                        remains of my life
in the old country and dumped them down into the
                                        eyes of the paranoid fish
of a dying, poisonous lake   I crept into the limbo
                                        of a hazardous geography
preparing my palms for the stings of curdling alms,
given to me by those who would make sure
it was their generosity that kept my sharpened hoofs
digging into my heart's ever-hardening grounds

2
How could anyone know of Kurdish mountains
Before movies were sent out to world festivals?
                                        What an irony!
They had been there even long before Dionysus was
                                        inspired
by their tambourine; long before Herodotus wrote
                                        the history
of the youth-killing king of Medes. We hurried to the
                                        top
in the snow that echoed in the hollows of the valleys
with the howling of wolves; and the teen girls

in veils crouched among men in rough sheepskins
                                          walking
on all fours, pretending that nothing human was
                                          happening,
even with the children crying and coughing and
                                          dying
—with eyelids of broken pieces of sleep betraying
                                  sad and innocent
pupils, depressed and pressed back into the corners
                                  of the sockets
And the wives sitting on the frozen crags
saying let them come and take us all, who cares for life
                                          or politics
or men married to stupid politics and pulling us along
                                          as they go
And reconnaissance was conducted at every ascent
                          and descent on the other side,
because down below, beyond the gutters of the valleys
in the opening with no buildings to give murder a
                                  context and a history,
they were preparing to shoot those who didn't make it
                                          to the top
where we stood. And was I destined to be the newly
                                  baked bread
to be broken into pieces among nations? Or was I
                                  the poet
clad in sheepskin to cross the border, refusing to go back
                                  and join the herd?
Or was I the poet, period? Then I heard the sound of
                                          the Daf,
the tambourine, played on top of the highest of mountains,
to all the Kurdish nation, fragmented into tribes in several
                                          countries
Then I heard the unanimous howling of the wolves to the
                                  echoing of the Daf,
And I stood up, walked out of the sheepskin to be pierced
by the crisscross of the bullets coming from the guards
                                  in the valley   But no,
they were shooting down there in the valley the ones who
                                  could not be with us
And now we were going down, not on all fours
this time, but running so fast that the world and the kids
in our arms and trails couldn't stop us
And the smugglers finally ready for their money

with strange smiles, only in their eyes
And then sitting in the Turkish village sipping the
                                    steaming chorba,
with the men counting the money and the women wiping
the runny noses of the kids
unaware of the deep continents of exile yawning under
                                    their feet
And already they were in it knee-deep, and soon it would
                                    be breast high
And suddenly someone remembering
One of the twelve men, standing before the firing squad,
with one hand cut-off for having stolen a guard's cap for
                                    cover
to cross to the other side. And the hand sniffed at by
                                    the dogs
but left untouched. Someone should be able to tell
the difference between the dogs and the guards

3

The only things I took away: a tattered coat
the parchment of these words carved by frozen fingers
                                    and knuckles
and these feathers, left over from forgotten birds
and these eyes as wide as three continents

When I lay down, I thought it was time for peace
Did I deserve it?
The tall sky covered with the nearest stars ever
The clouds moving past the moon
Birds singing all through the dawn
Women curled like thin hair around men and women
And bodies as softened swords

And slept, like a baby, thinking that I had just been born

Then I heard the turning of the keys
The coming of the walls
The rising of scorched faces
The familiar graves
And pitfalls that sped the measures of pain and space

The key in my fist, and the key in the garden where I left
when I left   withering in my mind in the water
in the gray rain, in the blood streaming through the wells

sinking through the leaves and trunks of trees
the sucked-in jaws of old men, the distorted mouths
                                          and teeth
the empty, hanging breasts of old women
the younger ones who were mine, and I, theirs
the key in my fist and the key in the garden of
                                  withered willows
where I left when I left never left and left

The dog that I was, yelping in the suburbs
of the last half of the last century   and the winds
                                    blowing all over
six millennia of deserts, wounds, shield, the cuneiform of
                                        half-truths
words of non-truth, the miracles of the breath and the
                                        sweat of
revolting wells of poems running into every corner of
                                        cities
the sponge of dreams invading everywhere, not knowing
Yes, the dog that I was, is now yelping on the streets of
                            Europe and America
With no end, no end.
And all because of the key in my fist, the same key that
                                        I left

Where I left when I left never left and left

In language that is not language
in words that are not words
caught in between saying and not wanting to say
at the threshold of not wanting to go back and
                              going back
going back and wanting to stay back here and not there
cutting my throat with this dagger, poetry

And suddenly I woke up and found the key in my hand:
The poem

2003

In the New Place, or Exile, a Simple Matter

In the new place you do not speak of yourself
    your feet facing the front
    you tread backwards with needles in your throat
The etched plot was there before you suddenly stepped in
The old place walks ahead of you
    someone claps his hands and then you have two husbands
    one forgetting you, the other not remembering
The distance walks away with you
      both in the new country, and the old one
You gather leaves, stuff them into your ears
      and pull up the blindfold, fearing you will be raped
                    in the eyes
You buy a new set of false teeth
      and write your brother at home to mail you a brand
               new false mouth
Instead, he sent you Discourses of Shams of Tabriz,
             Rumi's mentor,
Because time is ripe to write the Third Script:
    The one neither the scribe nor the reader will
             understand
"Shines
in the mind of Heaven   God
who made it
more than the sun
in your eye.
Fifth element; mud; said Napoleon"
After the explosion into incomprehension
    the unimpossible beauty you might call it
    (two negations equaling not affirmation
    but running the whole gamut of endless negation)
Pound dissolves words into meanings, and Shams says,
             "do not, I say"
But after the first four lines of Canto LI, Pound has already
             missed the point
    you hear him reading the rest of the poem
    four sets of false teeth blocking breath's rush to
             the mouth,
    giving reference and preference to history,
             missing the point once again

You are after Walter Benjamin's fasting man
    but who is fasting here?
You want to tell someone or write somewhere

that you find affinities between Shams and Benjamin too
both are pre-Adamite hermaphrodites in sudden languages
it hurts that no one knows
You buy a small bouquet of flowers
You're going to see your new boss
    clinging to the precipice of his imperial desk
And everyone is in search of something here
    they call it competence, and you call it
    the salad dressing of the new malady
They say you ought to have eye contact with everyone
    you have it with the beasts
    why not with the humans?

And you are the new talk of centuries
    both the old and the new
    and you have hoisted both of them on your shoulders

All hurt minds of both dark hemis
                  pheres
                  broke down into exile
    at home or abroad, etching with broken wrists
    what Benjamin called "a charmed circle of fragments."
And your small bouquet of flowers laughs at your hypocrisy
    you toss it away and you watch
    until it gets tossed back at you

Suddenly the word 'obfuscation' comes between you and the
                                         boss
    you see him sleeping while you are speaking
    eye contacting   and the birds in the yard
                chirp away in a frenzy, laughing at you
And you start telling your boss of the "fasting man
        who tells his dream as if…"
You stop, the boss is sleeping and you are scared
    scared that he will suddenly snore
And you won't know what to do with the malady of both
                        centuries,
The birds have stopped singing
    He wakes up as soon as you stop
    and says: "don't, don't bother the snoring, if I snore,
    I'm still listening."
And he closes his eyes, and you tell him about the word
                      'obfuscation,'
To decipher the obliterated cipher of your being and his

And "the fasting man who tells his dream as if he were..."
He suddenly wakes up and says: "be sure I'll do something
                                                    about it,
      but competence, don't forget competence..."
And Walter Benjamin says: "a charmed circle of fragments."

I was not asking for money.
It soils the hand that gives
      and the hand that takes
      but I do not tell him, I need a job, a better job, for sure
And this is not the question. I'm trying to have the eye
                                          contact going
      And I gauge competence
For this you need a new sort of concentration
Like the one you had when you were being born
Passing through someone in blood and pus, deaf and blind
      the concentration of a solid constipation
      the towering, excruciating empire of constipation
And then somebody slapping you hard, screaming
                                          'Obfuscation!'
And you opening your eyes to the world, recognizing
      that the boss has no snoring habits
He has the unfortunate habit of sleeping soundly only,
                                          yes only
      —this I won't tell you— but here it is anyway;
      only, when a writer in exile speaks
You don't know the new country for sure
      and now you hardly know the old one either
And you start again, with your only strength in the argument:
      "The fasting man who tells his dream as if he were
                                          talking..."
And the boss wakes up: "don't stop, I'm listening!"
      "But Sir, you're interrupting, I haven't stopped yet!"
I'm passing through mud and pus, deaf and blind
He sleeps now like a baby in a cradle
      on the grass on top of a cliff by the coast
      and the waves rolling with the white foam of their whales
                                          down there

"As I was saying..." I begin
And I stop in Benjamin's "charmed circle of fragments."
"I am not from the country, you know. I am just talking about
the fasting man who tells his dream as if he were talking in his
                                          sleep.

Comprenez? This is a country with two official languages!"
But there is some kind of innocence in this man's guilt
    as there is some kind of guilt in my innocence.

Now I am already for action.
I put my left hand in my pocket
    slowly,
    sexually
    surreptitiously
Remember Benjamin: "Your strength lies in improvisation.
    All the decisive blows are struck left-handed."
I open the blade of my knife in my pocket as he sleeps
    take out the knife
    the baby, oh the baby, in a cradle on the grass
    on top of a cliff by the coast, and the whales down there
                           in the waves
I need a test: is he awake when he is awake?
    Is he asleep when he is asleep?
    Is he awake when he is asleep?
    Is he asleep when he is awake?
    Is he, he?

So language tells you things that reality doesn't
I decide I'll wake him by telling him a funny story:
The woman says, you cannot do that here, it's impossible. She
cannot help but laugh. The old man is holding something
between his two hands. Kids passing by do not notice it. It's
only the shrewd eyes of the old woman that notices the vein-
stricken hands of the man holding *it* between them. Then she
says he shouldn't be ashamed of himself. He is genuine. Artistic.
Look at the young generation: they don't even know how to
hold *it* between their hands! She gets going but after a minute
she turns back to tell him he can hold *it* like that for as long as
he wants. But he has turned his back to her. And she doesn't
find the hairy back interesting at all. And then suddenly she
sees the front and back of the man at the same time, and her
own face with all the wrinkles reflected in the mirror, facing
both of them.

Is this the "charmed circle of fragments, Benjamin?" I scream
And when the boss wakes up to sneeze 'Obfuscation!'
    —dear reader or listener!
    "Hypocrite lecteur! —mon semblable—mon frère!—
    If you want to take a leak, please feel free to get up and

go and do so
This is not a practice in suspense poetry

I thrust the knife, with the same left hand
    drive it to the hilt into the heart
And fall supine before him, when he is rising
    not to call an ambulance,
but to answer the telephone that started ringing
    a minute before he was dead.

August 30, 2003
Toronto, Canada

Notes:
The six lines from Ezra Pound belong to Canto L1, The
Cantos of Ezra Pound (A New Direction Book, New York,
Eighth Printing, 1981) p. 250
The quotations from Walter Benjamin are:
"The fasting man who tells his dream as if he were talking in
his sleep."
"Charmed circle of fragments."
There are days when no one should rely unduly on his
"competence."
"Strength lies in improvisations.
All the decisive blows are struck left-handed."
They come from his selection called "One-Way Street" in
Walter Benjamin Reflections, ed. by Peter Demetz (New York,
Harcourt Brace Jovanovich, 1978), pages 62, 64, and 65.
The Benjamin quotations are sometimes used in fragmented
forms.
The French line is from Baudelaire's Les Fleurs du Mal,
meaning: "Hypocrite reader, my image, my brother!"

www.ingramcontent.com/pod-product-compliance
Lightning Source LLC
Chambersburg PA
CBHW032006040426
42448CB00006B/498